CW00921803

THE 28 DAY
SELF-ESTEEM
REBOOT

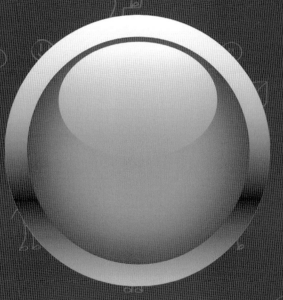

SUCCESS AND HAPPINESS
START WITH SELF-ESTEEM

GEORGE SWIFT

Copyright

Published by Bigger Brighter Bolder Publishing Ltd.
ISBN 978-1-9993333-9-3
Cover design by Annie Hall, Phase Two Design.
Printed in the UK

What Others Say

"The Self-Esteem Reboot was life
changing, and I can honestly say I
learnt more about myself in 28 days
than I had in my whole life up until
that point.

I went into it with no expectations,
thinking I'd probably come out having
improved my self-esteem a little.
What happened was incredible. It
is not easy - but then looking deep
inside yourself never is.

I'm definitely more confident and
braver than ever before off the back of this book, both
personally and professionally.

Thank you for showing me the way!"

- Kim Hughs

"Thank you! This has been the best detox I have ever done.
Through this, I've had to face the suppressed, forgotten
"demons" that were at the root of my self-esteem issues,
acknowledge them and move on. Not easy. A rollercoaster and
what a ride! I have a sense of peace that cannot be explained.
Just awesome!"

- Heide Cussell

"I've been really elated by the power of this Reboot! I knew that my self-esteem would benefit from a boost but what I got was so much more. The earlier lessons were prodding and analysing negative patterns, behaviours and beliefs. The latter lessons were more challenging and at times uncomfortable. The truth can be!

Looking back over the Reboot highlights, I'm amazed at some of my personal takeaways; moving away from negative people has had a bigger than expected impact, stopping trying to be perfect - it doesn't exist, and being more honest with myself - we all kid ourselves to "cover" our fears.

I'll continue to build upon the positive energy this Reboot has provided, thank you!"

- Clare Sheffield

"Hey George just wanted to say that I've just finished the self esteem reboot again and it's really been an incredible support and boost during a stressful period, so a massive thank you. It was like having a mini-George on my shoulder for 28 days, and it really kept my head in the right place.

- Tory Wagg

"I have been looking at my Before and After pages. Thank you for your many pearls of wisdom and helping me leap forward! The wonderful thing about your programme is that you speak from your own experience and learning, and that sharing is very powerful. Thank you!"

- Mandy Barter

"WTF... that totally took me by surprise! When I looked at the before and after comparisons, everything had greatly improved. My self-esteem went from 2/10 to 9/10. I hadn't even realised it until I went and filled in the comparison form. Quietly stunned and hugely appreciative. Many thanks!"

- Paul Hornsey-Pennell

"I've got myself into a lovely ritual of writing my highlights in the evening and doing the inspirational lessons in the morning. I can definitely see a difference as I'm really noticing my highlights now and making the most of them. This Reboot couldn't have come at a better time for me - I'm finding myself much braver and more positive towards my work. Thank you!"

- Anna Dora

"I've been meaning to message for over a week to say a huge thank you. I love the programme!! It wasn't all up. I had a slight dip around day ten, but I was still nailing the daily routine. By the end I felt so much better about myself. And I have continued. Really enjoy the daily commitment and it works! Love your lessons - spot on. Thanks!"

- Claire Dore

"Thanks for this amazing journey!! This has been so good for me and I'm reaping the benefits!!"

- Lisa Bedlow

"Really proud of myself to have committed to and completed the last 28 days on The Self-Esteem Reboot.

My self-esteem had taken a knock over the last couple of years through the early stages of motherhood - often single-parenting as my husband works away lots and I have very limited support around me. I love being a mum but the change in lifestyle, isolation and sleep deprivation has been challenging on many levels. My work, which I love, has been a juggling act for many months.
The 28-Day Self-Esteem Reboot has been a great way to shift the focus back onto me for a short time each day. As a result, I'm feeling much more confident in myself overall. I feel ready to step out again to promote my work. I'm also feeling more confident, present and loving as a mum, and enjoy all the little things this precious time brings. I feel great inside and excited for whatever is next. Thank you!"

- Janie Perry

"I've noticed that during the first week my emotions and energy levels were higher, which positively impacted my relationships. Also, I have become more aware of the opportunities around me that were always there but which I didn't always see.
My biggest breakthrough is realising that to be vulnerable is liberating and a strength. I'm looking forward to discovering further realisations as I progress through the 28 days."

- Sean Banning

"Thank you so much! I did it! I finished and I'm so glad I did. What an amazing journey! My biggest takeaway is understanding that it is completely possible to interrupt negative emotions and turn them around, and how important it is to look after yourself. It is so much harder to interrupt the negative emotions when you're physically tired!"

- Julia Blake

Contents

Dedication

This book is dedicated to my mum and dad, Dorothy and Mike. Mum, for always believing in the best of me and giving me the freedom to explore life without judgement. Dad, for being my greatest fan and for frequently telling me how proud he was of me.

Welcome

Welcome to The 28-Day Self-Esteem Reboot. I'm excited to share this programme with you. I first used this approach many years ago with my private clients, and with great success. Since then it has proven itself time and time again. Over the years I have witnessed that there is nothing which cannot be improved by having increased levels of self-esteem. It is the foundation of creating a healthy, happy and successful life.

You've purchased the book, now make it work for you. Make a commitment, right now, to see this through. It only takes a small investment of your time each day but sticking to it for 28 days is going to be challenging – not everyone will make it. Decide, right now, that you will be one of those who gets to the end. If you do, life will be better on the other side.

This Is So Much More Than A Book

The 28-Day Self-Esteem Reboot is a full four-week programme consisting of daily exercises, daily lessons and ongoing coaching. In order to get the most out of it, fully participate and engage with it. If you do, it will work for you, just as it has for everyone who has fully committed to it in the past. Don't let the small stature of this book fool you into not taking it seriously. I deliberately designed this book to be pocket-sized so that you could carry it with you discreetly throughout the day, should you wish to. It's a small book but it packs a mighty punch.

You can find a plethora of supporting material at: www.BiggerBrighterBolder.co.uk/Reboot/Resources - please check it out.

Thank you for participating in this programme, and good luck!

Introduction

Whilst this programme has been specifically designed to reboot your self-esteem and confidence, its lessons have far greater value. Think of it as a manual for creating the life you choose and living it on your terms – a self-empowerment handbook for living your best life as your best self.

Disclaimer

The 28-Day Self-Esteem Reboot is a process proven to encourage, develop and challenge greater levels of self-esteem and confidence. Whilst it has been specifically designed to be a gentle process, it could be too challenging for some.

This programme is not a replacement for professional counselling or therapy. If you believe you require the services of an appropriate professional, you should seek them out.

What Got You Here?

I'm going to assume that you're reading this because you are in one of the following places.

- It's possible you've had a little dip in self-esteem recently and you're looking to top it up.
- It's possible your self-esteem has taken a bit of a battering, either through one significant event or through multiple, smaller challenges.
- Maybe it's been a long time since you felt confident or good about yourself.
- Maybe you're feeling confident and your self-esteem is in great shape but you want to take it, and you, to the next level.
- It's also possible, of course, that you just thought, "Hey, this looks interesting. Let's just jump in and see what it's all about."

However we ended up together, I'm excited to have you on board.

What's In Store?

"This programme is split into two halves. The first half is predominantly about awareness. The second half is more focused on taking action and creating change. That's as much as I'm going to share with you right now. I don't want to give the game away.

You need to be patient and trust in the process. I've deliberately designed this programme to drip feed you what you need when you need it, in order to keep you on track to your final Reboot in 28-days time. Throughout the Reboot, I'll be asking you to lean against the status quo and I know that can be challenging. The journey we'll take is a process that has proven itself, time and time again. Stick with it and it will work for you too.

This programme is about personal empowerment. When we feel empowered to be who we want to be and live our life the way we feel is right for us, we can live a truly fulfilling existence. The education pieces in this programme are easy to digest and implement and will create the spark you need to transform your life.

So, don't read ahead or rush to the finish line. Take it one day at a time and stick with it. As long as you open this book each and every day and read that day's lesson, I will coach you every step of the way. Commit to that, especially on the days you don't want to, and I'll get you to the finish line.

I've created a suite of supporting materials to help you navigate the 28 days.

These include:

- a welcome video from me.
- multiple support videos to keep you engaged and tackle specific issues that might crop up and halt our progress.
- meditations and visualisations to speed up the Reboot process.
- other resources to support you on this journey.
- Plus, there is bonus content to unlock as you progress through the Reboot. The codes to access this content are hidden in this book. But don't worry, you won't miss them. They show up when the time is right.

You might want to go and familiarise yourself with these now. www.BiggerBrighterBolder.co.uk/Reboot/Resources

What Is Self-Esteem?

Think of self-esteem as your self-worth – the value you put on yourself. It's how much you like and approve of who you are. It's also your self-concept – your idea of who you are. It goes without saying that you want to have high levels of self-worth and have a strong self-image in order to live a successful and fulfilling life.

Success And Happiness Start With Self-Esteem

You can only get out of life what you deserve, and what you believe you deserve is set by your level of self-esteem. If you raise your self-esteem it enables you to have more scope, more potential and more possibility for achievement and happiness in life. Self-esteem affects everything from your confidence levels to your personal relationships and physical and mental health. It also sets the bar for how you're willing to be treated by others. People with high levels of self-esteem expect the best from themselves and don't tolerate being treated as any less valuable than they deserve. Those with low self-esteem expect little from themselves or from others and can expect little from life.

Self-esteem affects your ability to be assertive, your authenticity, how you present yourself to the world and your ability to create change. What you get back in life is determined by what you put out, and if you're not able to put yourself out there completely and fully then, of course, what you get back will be negatively affected. When you've got high levels of self-esteem you're in control of your life. You're free to determine who you are to the world and what you want to achieve, and you're able to go out and live that life.

How to Identify Whether You Have Lower Than Desired Self-Esteem

If you're reading this book because you're feeling your self-esteem isn't quite where it should be, you may relate to a number of the following negative impacts of low self-esteem.

- The acceptance of others' negative behaviour towards you.
- Allowing others to hold you back.
- Conforming to others' expectations or agreeing with

others' opinions even when it violates your own values or is detrimental to your needs and desires.
- Being a people pleaser.
- Being overly impacted by the criticism of others.
- Abdicating responsibility over decision making.
- Judging other people harshly or feeling the urge to criticise or put others down.
- Finding it hard to trust others.
- Struggling to accept love from yourself or others.
- Having a negative impact on other people.
- Presenting aggressive or defensive behaviour.
- Frequent frustration with yourself.
- Having a victim mentality – not taking responsibility for yourself and blaming others or external factors.
- Frequently feeling anxious.
- Having a low mood or feelings of depression.

Whilst there could be many potential underlying reasons why you might experience these, they are also all expressions and symptoms of low self-esteem. If you resonate with any of these and suspect low self-esteem as a potential cause, you're in the right place. This programme looks to reboot your self-esteem to optimum levels and, by default, improve life. Below, is a list of some of the benefits you might expect to see with your self-esteem fully rebooted.

- Full self-expression.
- Having trust in your decision making.
- Confidence which is not easily dented.
- Standing your ground and not being easily swayed.
- Being open to being wrong and being less stubborn.
- Being more comfortable in your skin and liking yourself.
- A sense of pride in yourself.
- Self-acceptance.
- Being more openly loving and more open to being loved.
- Saying "no" and meaning it.

- Growing in ambition and daring to dream big.
- Trusting in yourself more.
- Being more focused on your goals and agenda.
- Feeling happier.
- Feeling more optimistic.
- Being less stressed and anxious.
- Becoming more successful.

Positive self-esteem doesn't come from bullshitting yourself or being bullshitted by others into thinking or believing that you are better than you are. True, high levels of self-esteem come from a genuine, honest and authentic appreciation for who you are and for all that you do.

The 28-Day Reboot taps into the core fundamentals of deep-rooted expressions of positive self-esteem.

There's A Bonus

When you have high levels of self-esteem, you're like a magnet to others who also possess high levels of self-esteem. People with greater self-esteem are typically more fun, more supportive and nicer to be around. These people have no need to put anyone down and will only want you to succeed. Being around these go-getting, authentic souls will improve you and your quality of life. Equally, imagine tapping into the best, most positive version of yourself and think what a positive force you could be for those people close to you.

Don't Be Scared

If you are struggling with your self-esteem at the moment, it's possible that this all seems a little scary right now. It shouldn't and needn't be, but I get it. I, too, struggled with low self-esteem for many years. Even to this day, if I don't catch it creeping in it can still crop up and take me by surprise. It's why

I'm so passionate about this programme. For many years, in many guises, I've helped people with their self-esteem. Now I want to help you navigate your way to a happier and more fulfilling life.

The Fear Of Failure

The fear of failure is powerful. If you're doubting this programme is going to work for you, keep an open mind. You may be doubting the programme itself, in which case, know it has positively impacted every single person I have ever put through it. For some it proves to be truly transformational. It really will work for you too. If you believe in the programme but are doubting yourself, don't. Just follow along each day. Do what is asked of you and allow the 28 days to do their job. The only ways to fail at the Reboot are to not start it or not see it through.

If you commit to reading the lessons and completing the daily exercises, you'll be successful. Be open-minded about the process and where it takes you. Be open to what it unearths and don't be afraid to explore your life or yourself. Participate fully, even when you're doubting yourself or the process. I've followed this programme many times myself and it works. I truly believe it will work for you as well.

The Fear Of Change

The fear of change can often be greater than the fear of failure. You might be thinking, "What if this works? Who will I be? What will I want to do? What's going to change?" In fact, it's well documented that the fear of success is greater than the fear of failure because of our fear of change. We can therefore unconsciously resist positive change, even when it seems completely counterintuitive to do so.

Don't fear change. Our inability to accept change is what keeps us holding on too tightly to the many things in our life that are not good for us. You must trust in your better self. There are absolutely no negative effects of having high levels of authentic self-esteem and confidence. It's all good. Therefore, any change that comes about because of increasing your self-esteem and confidence must also be good. With your new-found, or re-found, self-esteem, you will want to create changes to your life. You may want to change specific parts of life, such as self-expression, career and work, or how people treat you. You might want to be generally happier or more fulfilled. It's normal to want to pick and choose where you want life to change. However, changing a specific area of life may also have a knock-on effect on other areas.

When you start improving your self-esteem, your current life isn't always as good a fit as it was, sparking an impulse to create greater change. But always remember, any change that comes from you having greater levels of self-esteem has to be a positive change, even if it's one that you wouldn't necessarily choose. Be brave.

The Fear Of Becoming A Knob

Sometimes, people mistake negative character traits such as arrogance, conceitedness and self-righteousness for high levels of self-esteem. Those character traits are actually more symbolic of low levels of self-esteem. People with genuine high levels of self-esteem simply don't behave like that. If you believe that high levels of self-esteem will turn you into some kind of arsehole, you'll hold yourself back from creating that change. You cannot have too high a level of self-esteem. The greater your self-esteem and confidence, the more positive and beneficial you'll be for yourself and others. You will not become a knob – quite the contrary. You'll lose negative aspects of your character and strengthen and develop the positive. You need to understand this because not everyone will see your change as positive. If, at any point, you experience negative reactions to your increased self-esteem, this only highlights an issue in them and has nothing to do with you.

Can You Trust Me?

Quite some time ago I was given the nickname, The Mindset Mechanic. I don't go by that anymore, but I do teach an understanding of what I still call Mindset Mechanics. Human behaviour can be broken down into mechanical processes. Like a mechanic who knows their way around an engine, you can troubleshoot the human mind and work out why it's not firing on all cylinders. Sometimes it only needs a tweak to the tuning, while at other times it needs a complete overhaul. I take complicated neurological processes and psychological concepts and deliver them in a way that makes them easy to consume, digest, and most importantly, apply.

I've got a great track record in helping people. I have over 25 years' experience in empowering individuals and teams and improving personal performance. I have been involved in inner-city rejuvenation projects, working with people who live under a constant threat of violence. I've also worked with the Prince's Trust and many high-profile businesses. In 2009, I founded Bigger Brighter Bolder (BBB). By focussing on the mindset, attitudinal, performance and cultural aspects of success, I have coached individuals, CEOs, senior executives, sales people and sports teams to significant levels of achievement.

I have successfully worked with people with eating disorders, self-harming, depression, anxiety, and violent and suicidal tendencies. I've helped them through the processes of understanding themselves and how they tick so that they can go on to create happy, successful and rewarding lives.

I have a passion for entrepreneurism and in 2012 I launched BBB Success Groups for ambitious business owners, through which I have coached and mentored over 500 businesses, including start-ups, one-man bands, six-figure businesses and multi-million-pound enterprises.

Struggling with my own confidence and self-esteem for so many years has given me insight into the positive and negative impacts of high and low self-esteem respectively – not just for success, but for happiness, fulfilment and overall quality of life.

I understand where you are right now and if ever I find my old negative habits around confidence and self-esteem creeping back in, this is the process I always come back to. And not just because it's mine, but because it bloody-well works – every time!

Your Workbook

As mentioned above, there's a Workbook that accompanies this programme. I've included it at the back of this book – it starts on page 159. If you don't want to spoil this book by writing in it, you can purchase separate workbooks at www.BiggerBrighterBolder.co.uk/Reboot/Resources.

That's where you'll also find the welcome and support videos, the visualisations, and other resources to support your Reboot. If you haven't done so already, go and check those out right now.

Jump in with both feet and enjoy the process. I'll see you on Day 1.

Day 1 – Getting Started

Welcome to your first day on The 28-Day Self-Esteem Reboot. Let's jump straight in and set up the next 28 days.

If you're not intending to use the workbook included at the back of this book, please visit www.BiggerBrighterBolder. co.uk/Reboot/Resources, where you can purchase separate workbooks. The workbook accompanies everything we're doing on this programme. And, if you haven't done so already, check out all of the other supporting resources available for you there.

Before And After

You're going to complete the Before page, on page 232 in your workbook.

The Before page is where you will take a snapshot of where your self-esteem and confidence are at present. Below, I've included a list of areas for you to consider. You don't need to use all of these and you can add anything you feel is relevant that's not included in this list. You want to be as specific as you can. Make this about you and your life and not a generic exercise. Only add areas that are important to how you feel about yourself. You'll naturally focus on the areas you're unhappy with but, if you want to, it's also okay to include areas you already feel good about.

Areas to consider:

- How you express yourself
- How authentic you feel you're being
- Confidence to speak up
- Confidence in decision making
- Self-doubts
- Negative self-talk
- Negative body image
- The extent to which you value yourself
- Your behaviours
- Your expectations and ambitions

Then ask yourself the following:

- How is your self-esteem right now?
- How is your self-confidence?
- How are your levels of self-esteem presenting themselves at the moment?
- How do you feel about yourself?
- To what degree do you like yourself?
- What is your view of life?

Now complete the Before page, making notes of all relevant observations. Take as much time as you need but don't overthink it. You may have five or six notable things, or dozens. There's no right or wrong. Make notes to capture your starting point and we'll review in 27 days to see how far you've come.

Tracking Progress

You'll also be checking in on your progress at the end of each week. To do that, you first need to set the scale you'll be measuring yourself against and your starting point.

Turn to Setting Your Scale in your workbook on page 229.

On this page, you're going to create a scale to measure your self-esteem and confidence against. You will use the same scale throughout the 28 days. In the first section, write down a few bullet points or sentences that describe what zero out of ten would look like to you, where zero is the worst you can imagine your self-esteem and confidence could be.

Now consider what a ten would look like for you, where ten is the best you could possibly imagine for yourself. Again, write in bullets or sentences in the space provided. Remember, you cannot have too much confidence and self-esteem. Also remember that traits such as arrogance and conceit are symbolic of low self-esteem. A high level of self-esteem presents itself as self-assuredness, confidence, a sense of certainty, an authentic love for oneself, knowing one's own mind, and expressing oneself honestly and fearlessly.

People with high levels of self-esteem don't have to force it. It comes naturally to them. They're not necessarily big characters or powerhouse personalities and they're not overbearing. They may be quiet people but ooze charisma. They have faith in themselves and confidently share their opinions while remaining humble and having bags of humility.

Score Yourself

Based on the scale you've just set, draw a line on the Starting Point scale on the same page, illustrating where you are at this present time. You can score yourself in half increments if you want a greater degree of accuracy.

Try to be as objective as possible. You might be tempted to be unfairly hard on yourself if you feel you're not where you want to be. Equally, you might be tempted into scoring yourself higher than you are in order to make yourself feel better. Try to be as honest with yourself as possible and don't get caught up in how you feel about your score. It will go up over the 28 days.

Next, make a few comments in the space provided next to the scale as to why you have scored yourself as you have. This may make reference to the descriptions in your zero-to-ten scale and include any other assessment you've made in deriving your current score.

You'll be updating your progress in a similar way at the end of each week. The zero-to-ten scale will stay the same. You'll need to fight the temptation to move the goalposts as you improve as this cheats you out of appreciating the progress you will have made.

Remembering What You Need To Remember

Remembering what you need to remember when you need to remember it is one of the toughest but most important aspects of creating change. For example, everyone remembers they're on a diet when lying in bed at the end of the day. However, they needed to remember it when they made breakfast, bought lunch and prepared dinner. They need to remember it when they go food shopping, open their cupboards or access the fridge.

It'll be easy to forget what you learn on this programme but remembering is essential if you want to make progress. I've given you Reminder pages right at the front of your workbook to capture these important notes as you progress through the 28 days. It might be something poignant you read in one of the daily lessons. Maybe it's a thought or realisation you have at some point. Whatever you think is important to remember, make a note of it on these pages.

Priming Your Day

Throughout the Reboot I will prompt you to look at this list of reminders – I suggest you do this every morning to get your day off to a flying start. When we roll out of bed without an agenda we end up reacting to life in habitual ways. Those habitual patterns are what got us to where we are today. If we want to create change, we need to think, do and be different. By taking a few minutes every morning to go through your list of important reminders, you prime yourself to be on your agenda. If you forget what you need to remember one day, that's okay because you'll remind yourself the next. Over the course of the 28 days you will condition yourself with those important reminders and they will become part of who you are. Place this book and your workbook, if you're using a separate one, somewhere where you'll see it first thing in the morning and then as a prompt throughout the day.

To set your day up in the best possible way, you might also want to read the daily lessons first thing in the morning. Some days I might add a challenge to take action on. If now is the time to act on any of these lessons, do so. If it isn't, that's okay as well. Go through the Reboot at your own pace. You can always come back to any particular lesson and apply it at a future date. Nothing I share should be taken as prescriptive. You must choose for yourself if you are ready to take any specific action. Be mindful of the daily lessons but do as much or as little as you feel is appropriate for you at this time. Your confidence will grow with these challenges over the 28 days.

Visualisations

I've created meditations and visualisations to accompany this programme. I understand that these won't be for everyone but give them a listen before you write them off. They're designed specifically to ingrain many of the lessons contained within this book and I encourage you to listen to them as often as you can. You can choose which you do and when you do them. Some will prefer the morning, finding it a great way to set up their day. Others might choose to listen at night as they wind down for bed. Personally, I just listen when I want a short, quiet time of reflection, regardless of the time of day. If you don't get on with them initially, give it a few more attempts. If you still don't enjoy them, put them to one side and see if you fancy trying again at some point in the future. Not listening to the meditations or visualisation will not harm your progress through this programme. However, if you do get on with them and listen regularly, they can offer a boost to the Reboot. You can listen to them at:
www.BiggerBrighterBolder.co.uk/Reboot/Resources.

I Like Myself Because...

At the heart of the Reboot is the daily *I Like Myself...* exercise. Every day has a page in the workbook, starting with today – Day 1. I've designed a simple three-step process for uncovering what you authentically and honestly like about yourself. Each day, I challenge you to come up with at least three I Like Myself... statements. You'll see space for four in your workbook but if the mood takes you, make a note of as many as you can. As you become comfortable with the exercise it will be tempting to shortcut the process for uncovering these statements, but don't. Follow the process to the letter on day 28 just as you will later today – it's a big part of why this programme works.

It's too easy to make up stuff that we like about ourselves or to think about what we should like about ourselves. You might also default to known aspects of yourself you do genuinely like, but this process works by uncovering secrets about yourself you might not yet know. We are also looking for patterns which will become important in the second half of the Reboot.

Don't Cheat The Process

At the end of each day, turn to the corresponding page in the workbook and complete the *I Like Myself...* exercise in the following way.

First reflect on the highlights of the day. What were the best things that happened? Remember, you're aiming for three but you're not limited to that. Don't jump ahead or think too hard about it, just note the standout moments of that day.

In the first space provided, write what the highlight was and why it stood out for you.

Next, ask yourself what part you played in that highlight and write that in the second space. Some highlights will be more obvious than others – for example, if you gave a great presentation at work or achieved something notable. Other days it might be more challenging, perhaps receiving a gift or a compliment from someone. Maybe your highlight was sitting in a park and feeling at peace with the world. These highlights still required you to be a part of them. You played your part in that moment. Maybe it's being the type of person others like to do nice things for. Maybe you do nice things for other people and they repay those gestures. In the example of sitting in the park, maybe your part is that you have the capacity to observe and acknowledge the beauty in the world. Even if it feels you didn't play a part in the highlight, it's important you unearth your role in it.

Lastly, ask yourself what it is you like about yourself with regards to the highlight. The clue will be in the previous two steps. Once you have identified that, complete the sentence, *I Like Myself Because...* and write it in the final space provided. It may resemble what you've written in the My Part section or it might prompt something different. For example, "I like myself because I'm a nice person who other people choose to do nice things for." Or it might be as simple as, "I like myself because I'm thoughtful and considerate." Go with the process and see what comes up for you.

I Know This Might Be Challenging

Remember, I've also suffered significantly with my self-esteem in the past. At times I've truly despised who I was and the idea that I could like myself would have been incredibly challenging. Try not to overly engage with that part of you that feels uncomfortable with this process, especially the last part where you declare what you like about yourself. Don't listen to the voice in your head – follow the process, be brave, and acknowledge what you bring to the table of life and what you like about yourself because of it. Even if you struggle initially to connect with the I Like Myself... statement, write it out and acknowledge it. As is the case with anything, the more you do this the easier and more comfortable it will become. Your increasing comfort in following this process will be a clear signal to you that your self-esteem is rebooting.

Stick With It – It Really Works

There will be days where you'll struggle to find highlights, the part you played, or to tap into what you like about yourself. Those are the days that really matter. The harder they are to find or the more your subconscious resists, the greater the gains will be for following through. When we don't want to do something, or find it hard to do, we have the greatest opportunity for creating change.

Don't Let Your Subconscious Bullshit You Out Of Your Success

At times you may hear a little voice in your head that puts you down and tries to talk you out of this process. It might sound like a comforting voice saying you should take it easy on yourself and not put yourself through this. It might show itself as anger towards the process or towards me. It might be critical and judgemental of you, telling you you're not good enough or how this won't work for you. You might be some way down the line with the Reboot and have a bad day or two, with the little voice trying to convince you to give up because it's clearly not working.

Don't beat yourself up for having these thoughts, most people will have them at some point during the Reboot. Equally, don't pay too much attention to them. Unless you genuinely feel that the process is uncovering deep-rooted issues or stirring things up in a way that you can't handle, stick with it. If it becomes genuinely too uncomfortable you may need to stop. It's okay, maybe this isn't the right time for you to be taking on this Reboot. Instead, you might want to seek the help and support of a relevant qualified professional to help you navigate what's come up for you.

You'll become familiar with the patterns of language and tone of this inner critic. You can engage light-heartedly with it by saying something like, "Of course you'd say that," or, "I knew you'd have something to say about this." Always have the thought with a slight smile on your face. This totally disempowers the thought patterns that may have detrimentally dominated your life. But don't expect this impact to be immediate – be patient. There's a reason this Reboot takes place over 28 days.

Take Action

If there's anything you've just read you think you need to remember moving forward, add it to the Reminders on page 162 in the front of the workbook now. You can keep adding to this at any point during the next 28 days.

Tonight, before you go to sleep, complete the Day 1, *I Like Myself...* exercise on page 170. Challenge yourself to come up with three highlights and take the time to follow the process outlined above. Don't cheat it or shortcut it. And remember, the harder it is on any given day, the greater the benefits will be.

If you are confused about any of the above, please check out the supporting material online. I have created a Getting Started video that explains everything. Please visit: www.BiggerBrighterBolder.co.uk/Reboot/Resources.

Don't read ahead. I'll see you tomorrow for Day 2.

DAY 2 – The Link Between Self-Esteem And Success

26 Days Until Reboot

Welcome to Day 2 of The 28-Day Self-Esteem Reboot.

Recap

How are you getting on so far? Have you added anything to your Reminders page? Don't forget to add anything from these daily lessons that feels important to you. Also, add any personal revelations you might have as you go through this process. You want to reflect on your Reminders page first thing in the morning and ideally throughout the day. Remember that the more you remember what you need to remember when you need to remember it, the easier it will be to create change. For example, if you need to remember to speak more kindly to yourself, there's no point remembering that at the end of the day. You want to remember that at the time you're doing it or, ideally, just before you are about to do it. Constantly reminding yourself of what you need to be mindful of as you go through your day makes it easier to change any unwanted behaviours or thought patterns. Likewise when you're trying to instil new, more positive thought patterns and behaviours. Frequency is key.

Did you come up with at least three highlights last night? How comfortable were you with the process? Don't worry if it feels difficult or weird. The more you do it, the easier and more enjoyable it will become. If you found it easy, great! But don't let the fact you found it easy diminish the power this little exercise has to create deep-rooted, long-term change. Don't forget to complete Day 2 in your workbook tonight. Remember, the harder it is to find these highlights, and the subsequent *I Like Myself...* statements, the more important it is to find them.

Make this one of the last things you do every night – you'll sleep on it and it will set up the next day to be more positive.

Success Starts With Self-Esteem

I didn't create this programme simply to make you feel better, despite that being a worthwhile endeavour in itself. Instead, I want this programme to form the foundations for you to build your future success upon.

Having worked in the field of personal performance for many years, including helping business owners achieve success, I've witnessed the direct link between self-esteem, confidence and success.

Our subconscious sets the bar for what we are able to achieve. Low self-esteem limits what we feel we deserve and what we feel we deserve limits what we can achieve. If we want to achieve more, we need to raise that bar. This self-limiting relationship between self-esteem and success shows itself in all areas of life. Wealth, health, relationships and happiness will all reflect your level of self-esteem.

Raising The Bar

You don't use all your strength when opening a jar, you use the amount you have learned is required. Your subconscious programming dictates how much strength and commitment you bring to the task. You do the same in all areas of life. Your programming manipulates what result you expect in each situation. Your subconscious then brings the level of energy, focus and commitment it has learned is needed in order to get the expected result. Therefore, what you expect to get out of life is often exactly what you do get.

If you start to get more than you have learned you deserve you will likely sabotage yourself back to levels you subconsciously find more comfortable. Think of this process like the thermostat on your central heating. If the room gets warmer than the temperature the thermostat is set at, the heating automatically switches off until the room falls below the set level. Your level of deserving acts as an internal thermostat that stops you overachieving by manipulating your thoughts, feelings, actions and behaviours.

If you have high levels of self-esteem, you feel you deserve more and generally have much higher expectations. By improving your self-esteem, you raise the bar for what you deserve and expect and, in doing so, subconsciously align your actions and behaviours to obtain that improved result. Additionally, improved self-esteem improves confidence, enabling you to express and exert yourself in more empowering and positive ways, leading to greater success. Conversely, low self-esteem lowers your confidence levels and limits your ability to have impact on your world.

The Self-Esteem Reboot is designed to rebuild and strengthen the foundations of your self-esteem to enable you to build your successful life. Whether you want to create a successful business, improve your relationships, be happier, or you want an all-round fulfilling life, boosting your level of self-esteem is an absolute must.

Success (and happiness) starts with self-esteem.

Add anything important to your list of Reminders on page 162 and make sure you complete the Day 2, *I Like Myself...* exercise on page 172 tonight.

Don't forget to come back for more tomorrow.

DAY 3 – Permission To Protect Yourself

25 Days Until Reboot

First things first – a little friendly reminder. Are you completing your workbook? You won't get the results you want if you don't participate fully with the exercises.

A fundamental part of creating change, as I have already said, is remembering what it is you need to remember when you need to remember it. Therefore, the first thing you should've done this morning is jump straight to your Reminders on page 162 and go through any notes you've made about what it is that you need to be remembering as you continue on the 28-Day Reboot. You'll build this up over time.

Don't forget, as you head to bed tonight you're going to complete Day 3 of your workbook and complete the *I Like Myself...* exercise on page 174. Take a moment afterwards to connect with this and drift off to sleep, peacefully liking yourself.

Permission Granted

You should consider giving yourself permission to protect yourself for the duration of this Reboot. In an ideal world, you would be impervious to other people's judgement, criticisms and unwanted feedback. But, the chances are you don't have those levels of resilience right now.

Having high levels of self-esteem is like wearing a suit of armour. When you're at your most confident, strong and self-assured, people and life can throw anything at you and it will simply bounce off. When your self-esteem is low, every single one of those attacks puts another dent in your armour. If there are any chinks in that armour you can be sure they'll find their way through.

This process is designed to strengthen your self-esteem – eventually to the point where you feel confident in expressing yourself fully in every aspect of life. But in order to repair any damage you've sustained to your armour you need to temporarily stay out of harm's way.

Choose Who You Spend Time With

Give yourself permission to reduce your exposure to those people who will limit your ability to do what it is that you're trying to do here. Be mindful who you share this experience with. You don't want to be sharing this journey with anyone who's going to piss on your fire or who thinks you're stupid or foolish for doing this. They may not be trying to harm or hurt you, but you really don't want to be sharing this experience with anyone who's going to negatively impact your ability to get the most out of these 28 days.

It's okay to temporarily stay clear of, or at least limit your exposure to people who are triggers for you feeling less than optimally about yourself. These people probably mean no harm but they will make this Reboot feel a little like pushing a boulder uphill. Make life easier on yourself – protect yourself for a while. If they're close family members this will be difficult. Even though you love them and will continue to love them, you won't want to let them get too close to what you're doing here. If they're friends, acquaintances or work colleagues, keep them at arm's length and limit your exposure to them and, with the worst offenders, remove them completely if possible.

If you're connected to people on social media who are negative around you or make you feel worse about yourself, block them. Either block them for good (why wouldn't you?) or at least block them for the next 25 days.

If you are fortunate enough to have people in your life who will support you on this journey and who are going to breathe life into your Reboot, I encourage you to share this experience with them.

Stay Away

Be mindful of environments that trigger negative feelings about yourself. You might find that you go to certain places where you feel worse, or which highlight your less-than-perfect self-esteem. These might not necessarily be negative places, they may simply be environments that bring out the worst in you. Maybe it's a place where you feel you can't be truly honest or authentic and you feel worse about yourself for putting on the charade. Again, there'll be a time when these places will have little negative impact on you, but for now, stay away and give yourself time to grow.

Maybe Take A Goals Sabbatical

Setting goals focuses the mind, directs action and is well proven to be a fundamental part of success and achievement. Goals can also boost self-esteem and confidence levels as you achieve what you set out to achieve. But consider temporarily steering clear of goals, targets and tasks that you are likely not to succeed at. For the time being you want to protect yourself from the experience of failure. Remember, this isn't forever. You'll want to get back to challenging yourself soon enough – it's healthy and productive – but maybe take a short break whilst you're in this process.

You cannot be successful without failing sometimes. A massive part of success is failing and daring to fail. When your self-esteem is robust you will be able to handle failure. Failing without experiencing negativity causes no damage. But while you might be feeling a little vulnerable, failure can get in the way of rebooting your self-esteem. For the purposes of this 28-Day Reboot I want you to limit the chances of feeling like 'a failure'.

Unless you have low self-esteem in all areas of life, you may pick and choose where you continue to set goals and targets. Goals in areas of life where you feel confident could actually enhance your experience of the Reboot, but choose wisely, and if in doubt, leave it out.

Don't Make Promises You Can't Keep

Don't make any promises or commitments you can't keep or which you'll resent. Doing so might damage your ability to create the change you're trying to achieve here. A large part of this process is the healing that needs to happen alongside personal growth and development. Giving yourself permission to protect yourself from those things that could cause damage to your self-esteem gives you the space to heal from previous harms. People pleasers often say yes to things in an attempt to feel good about themselves or make people like them. Sometimes they promise and commit to things they can't deliver, resulting in overwhelm and feeling bad about themselves. It's hard for some people to do, but give yourself permission to say no to other people and things where there's the risk of this.

Beware Criticism

Don't solicit feedback or criticism unless it's in an area of your life where you're confident. If you do seek feedback on anything you're not rock solid on, make sure it's from someone who you really trust and who's critical feedback, should it come, won't leave you feeling hurt in any way. The safest route for the next 25 days is to not solicit criticism or feedback at all. Don't ask for people's opinions if you might not like what they have to say. You're rebuilding your self-esteem and you don't want to slow this process down.

Stepping Out Of The Ring

Imagine a boxer in a fight, fresh and strong. His opponent throws some punches his way. He's ducking and diving and dodging the attack. He gets hit with a decent punch but it barely registers. Then comes another, and another. That last one stung a little. His legs feel a little weaker. The next punch lands clean and he feels his legs wobble. He's slowing and his arms are dropping. His guard is down and more and more of his opponent's punches are finding their target. He keeps fighting on. It's brave but foolish and the writing is on the wall – this fight is only going one way. His opponent hits him flush on the jaw and it's lights out.

Just as in boxing, life throws punches our way. Occasionally we get hit with a huge right hand, seemingly from nowhere, and it takes us off our feet. More often than not, life throws a succession of jabs and crosses - little things that by themselves don't cause too many problems. But if we don't get a break, these little hits build up and start to take their toll. The weaker we get, the less able we are to recover and protect ourselves. It might feel brave to stand there, toe-to-toe, taking punch after punch, but the smart fighter knows when to get out of the ring – to rest and recuperate and build back to full strength. Then they can come back stronger than ever and fight for the title.

There's no shame in needing a break from the fight. Use the

next 25 days to protect yourself so that you can heal and come back stronger than ever, too.

Exercise

Before you head off, grab a pen and answer the following questions.

- Which people make you feel worse about yourself?
- Which places make you feel worse about yourself?
- Are any of your goals and targets setting you up to fail?

Now decide how best to protect yourself for the remainder of this Reboot. Give yourself permission to step out of the ring and allow yourself the space and time needed to heal and grow. Add notes to your list of Reminders.

Finally, before you go to bed tonight don't forget to go to Day 3 of your workbook, follow the process and write down why you like yourself today.

DAY 4 – Be Patient And Trust Things Are Improving

24 Days Until Reboot

Have you kept up with your workbook? Did you take a good look at your Reminder pages first thing this morning? Have you been adding to that list as important things come up for you? It's important you do and, if you have been, by now you may be starting to collect some significant notes for yourself. Maybe you need to remember that you can achieve great levels of self-esteem. Or, remember that whatever difficulty you're going through is only temporary. Maybe you need to remind yourself of the people and places to avoid, and where to spend time and who with. Be consistent and systematic during this entire process.

You should also now have three days' worth of the *I Like Myself...* exercise completed and tonight, before you go to bed, you're going to do Day 4. Remember to aim for at least three every night. The more difficult it is to do, the more important it is for you to do it and the more benefit exists from completing the task. Don't shortcut the process, no matter how familiar or tempting it gets. Always do the exercise one step at a time – when you start the second half of the programme you'll thank me for this.

Anything Changing Yet?

Don't worry if it isn't, there's plenty of time left on the programme. However, it's possible you've already started getting little moments of feeling better about yourself. Maybe you've started seeing yourself and the world a little more optimistically. Equally, you may have been challenged by some of the content or exercises and it's possible that you may actually feel a little worse than you did when you started. That's okay, too.

Improvement is rarely linear and the journey you are on may feel a little up and down, especially in the beginning. No matter where you are currently, positive change is already happening. You need to be patient, trust in this process and commit for the entire 28 days.

Change IS Happening

I want you to imagine that your old way of thinking and being is protected by a layer of concrete. By interacting with this content and following the exercises, you're pouring new thinking and perspective all over that concrete. By excavating those little gems from the *I Like Myself...* exercise and constantly reviewing your Reminders, you are beginning to create change. You just might not be aware of it yet. Concrete is barely porous and most of this new positive thinking and awareness may be running off the surface. But some is making its way through.

Like water slowly breaching concrete, at first almost all of the new ideas may just run off. But more will make their way through as you continue the pouring of positive thinking and new perspective onto this layer. When a path through is finally created, more and more will flow through that channel. As it does, the channel will widen, allowing even more to flow.

This is the process we're beginning and why you may or may not be starting to feel the positive effects.

As you progress through the 28 days, you'll continue pouring more positivity and new perspective onto and through that concrete. For some, their subconscious and the issues they're dealing with aren't that set in stone. In their case, the new thinking will be starting to make its way through and they'll already be feeling better about life and themselves. For others, their concrete is a little thicker and less porous and they might not feel any change as yet. Either way, as the image of water pouring on concrete illustrates, change is already happening. Consistency and patience are the order of the day.

Changing The Fuel In Your System

You could look at this another way. Imagine the system fuelling your confidence and self-esteem is currently running on red fuel. This system includes your current thinking, perceptions and behaviours. If red fuel represents your old patterns of low self-esteem and blue the desired way of being, you want to replace the red fuel with blue fuel.

Unfortunately, you can't drain all the red fuel and replace it with blue instantaneously. By reading a lesson every day and following through with the exercises and challenges I set, you are slowly bringing more and more blue fuel into the system. At first you might barely notice the red changing colour but over time you will start to see the system turning a little purple. When you see and feel this shift, there'll be a new sense of belief in your ability to create change which, in turn, will accelerate the process. Momentum and motivation will build and you will be well on your way to turning your system completely blue, rebooting your self-esteem and confidence.

In my experience, the hardest weeks on the Reboot can be

weeks one and four. Week one because you're often running purely on faith, needing to trust that change is happening even though it might be impossible to see. Week four because by the end of week three you will be feeling better about yourself and might think you've done enough. You won't have but I'll explain that at the appropriate time.

Stick with the Self-Esteem Reboot. As long as you do, change is always happening whether you can see it or not. When you see and feel change, take time to acknowledge it – maybe as an *I Like Myself...* for that day. Today, regardless of whether you feel the same, better or worse, you should definitely like yourself because you are creating the changes that are bringing about the new, improved, confident you – complete with high levels of self-esteem.

Don't forget to do your *I Like Myself...* exercise and I'll see you back here tomorrow.

DAY 5 – Surround Yourself With Positivity

23 Days Until Reboot

As we approach the end of the first week it's important that you continue to trust in this process, even if your progress is not obvious to you yet. Please continue to do the daily exercises otherwise the Reboot will not work. Did you go to the Reminder page this morning? If not, stop reading and head over there now to remind yourself of what you need to be mindful of today. Then continue reading.

Positive People

Be in the presence of individuals that breathe life into you. I want you to surround yourself with the people who make you feel good about yourself.

Good people to be around are:

- those you can just be yourself around;
- those you feel most authentic around;
- those you feel most confident and at ease with;
- those you're able to fully express yourself around;
- those whose criticism or judgement you don't fear;
- those you have the most fun with and bring you the most joy.

I want you to deliberately spend more time with these people. You might want to add their names to your list of Reminders.

External Validation

We all seek a degree of external validation. It's inbuilt in us – it's one of our evolutionary human needs. Looking back to our tribal past, the external validation of others meant we were a valued member of those primitive societies. If we were valuable to our tribe, our tribe would take care of us and we were safe. That desire to please and to be accepted by others continues with us to this day. However, relying too heavily on external validation is a fallible strategy for building your self-esteem. Like a house of cards, it doesn't take the removal of much of that validation to potentially bring your whole self-esteem tumbling down.

You don't want to be relying on the external world to feel good about yourself on the inside. It's perfectly alright to accept and enjoy the validation of others when it's on offer and to use it to bolster your self-esteem, but you don't want to need it. However, certainly for the duration of the Reboot, it can be of great support. So use the time you've created through distancing yourself from negative people and environments, from Day 3, and invest it in those that fit the criteria above.

As stated already, a big part of this programme is the healing process. The growth phase will follow. I want you to spend time with those people who make you feel good about yourself – those who validate you as a human being, support you, don't judge or criticise you, love you just for who you are, and who you feel you can be your most authentic self around. You won't need to overly rely on this sort of validation once your self-esteem is fully restored but for now you're going through a process where it's okay to lean on this support.

Positive Environments

It's important to recognise which places are healthiest for you. Make a note of your answers to the following questions.

- Where do you feel best about yourself?
- Where do you feel most comfortable and relaxed?
- Where do you feel strongest and most confident?
- Which environments bring you the most joy?

Saturate Yourself In Positivity

Maximise your exposure to the positive people and environments you've identified in this lesson. Keep away from those which might damage your self-esteem. You might need to make some changes to your usual routine. For example, if going to the gym makes you feel good about yourself, spend time at the gym. However, if you go to the gym and it makes you feel lousy, consider not going for the duration of this programme. Instead, exercise in the privacy of your own home or somewhere that's more positive for you. If you keep intending to exercise but don't get around to it and that makes you feel negative, go easy on yourself and maybe let yourself off the hook for a while.

Make a note of positive changes you can make that will support you throughout the remainder of this Reboot.

Rebooting Now For The Future

You won't need to protect yourself forever. Once you have solid levels of self-esteem you'll be able to safely go to the places where you're not entirely comfortable. In the future you might need to be around people who are critical or judgemental and after the Reboot, you'll be strong enough to handle them.

However, if you start to feel vulnerable, always remember the lessons in this programme.

Add anything you need to remember from today's lesson to your list of Reminders and don't forget, before you go to sleep tonight, think of at least three highlights and complete the *I Like Myself...* exercise.

See you tomorrow.

DAY 6 – Changing Your Perspective Changes Your Reality

Today is about changing your perspective and how this can literally change your reality. This is a massive subject. However, for the purposes of the Reboot there are just a few things that you need to know.

Negative Feedback Loops

Outward expressions of low self-esteem will include things such as criticism of yourself and others, people pleasing, violating your own values, using controlling behaviours, lack of ambition, and lack of commitment and follow-through.

When you express yourself from a place of low self-esteem it presents itself in negative ways. When you witness yourself behaving negatively you feel worse about yourself – further lowering your self-esteem.

Feedback Loops Go Both Ways

Outward expressions of high self-esteem will include things such as the following.

- Compassion
- Patience with yourself and others
- Forgiveness of yourself and others
- Self-trust and trusting in others
- Positive self-reflection
- Being at ease with yourself
- Having nothing to prove
- Ambition, commitment and achievement

The more you observe these positive expressions of high self-esteem, the better you feel about yourself and your self-esteem grows.

You want to slow down and halt your negative feedback loops whilst accelerating and maximising the positive ones.

Perspective
The Angle From Which You Observe

Your perspective can be described as the angle from which you view yourself, others and the world around you. How you see these things will determine the reflection of reality you perceive. We all have the ability to negatively distort what we are observing by developing habitual negative ways of seeing things. Just like all habits, we can alter them by deliberately and consciously choosing our focus, reactions and behaviours.

The easiest way of breaking into these habitual patterns is through altering how you choose to see yourself and the world around you, thus altering the reflection of reality you are perceiving. The more positively you view life and the representation of yourself in it, the more you will naturally express yourself positively. This positive interaction with the world around you will make it much easier to see the good in you and it, and in turn it will reflect positively on your self-esteem and confidence.

Perception
The Filter Through Which You Observe

Perception is the filter through which you see yourself, others and the world. If you were looking at the world through a sheet of red-tinted glass, only red light would pass through it and therefore everything would be perceived as red. If you're running on red fuel (as described on Day 4), you're seeing yourself and the world through the red filter of low self-esteem.

With this negative filter in place it's very hard to see the positives. You may not have known you were viewing yourself and life through a filter, but now that you do you can consciously choose to see differently.

When you positively alter the perspective and perception of yourself and life, you both see and interpret these differently – reality alters and you begin creating a positive feedback loop.

Objective VS Subjective Reality

Objectivity means lacking favouritism, bias and judgement. Subjectivity is the opposite. We would agree on objective reality but might argue about subjective reality. For example, we might all agree a coffee mug is orange but we might disagree on whether that is a pleasant colour. Objectively, the mug is orange. Subjectively, its colour is pleasant or unpleasant. Our reaction to the mug will be based far less on its objective qualities and much more on our personal, subjective perspective.

To open up the possibility of creating substantial change, you must first understand that the reality you perceive of yourself, life and others is not an objective one. In fact, it is a very subjective reality, personal to you. Your past experiences dictate how you see yourself and life, and through what filter.

You think, act and react in alignment with your subjective bias towards yourself and the world around you. Low self-esteem distorts how you see yourself and puts disempowering filters in front of life. You want to remove those filters which lower your self-esteem. What you see as reality is not the only reality.

Dare To Be Wrong

Simply put, you have to dare to be wrong. You might perceive yourself as less than you are and make the mistake of believing that is real. Maybe someone in your past made you feel less than you are and you made that your reality, believing it to be true. It's possible you have objectively behaved poorly or negatively, but the mistake you made was thinking that these behaviours define who you are.

See Yourself In Increasingly Positive Ways

You must continually challenge yourself to see the world and yourself in increasingly positive ways.

Now you can see the importance of why you're doing the *I Like Myself...* exercise every day and why it's essential you continue to do so. Take pride in what you uncover about yourself. Don't make the mistake of thinking you're responsible for all the crap in your life but somehow got lucky with the good stuff.

Start taking time to acknowledge the part you play in your life and the world – the goodness, the greatness, the joy and the happiness that you bring. Even if you're not a massive ray of sunshine right now, look at the various aspects of who you are and start to notice more of the good. The more you see, the more you'll be able to see and you'll build momentum in that positive feedback loop. Also, seek out more of the good in the world. The more good you see, the better you will feel, helping you to see even more. You want to build that upward spiral. No one can do it for you – you need to commit to the process.

Exercise

What are some of the negative patterns you express that fuel your negative feedback loop?

You might have repeating negative patterns in how you perceive yourself or behave and express yourself. Maybe it's how you judge other people. Or maybe it's how you see the bad in the world or focus on what's threatening or scary in it.

Grab pen and paper and give some thought to the main undesirable habits that you've picked up.

- What are they?
- What new thought patterns, perspectives and filters do you need to put in place to counter them?

Pick one, two, or more, and add them to your list of Reminders so that you can begin breaking those patterns. Trust the process. As you start to block the negativity and begin to build on the positivity, you will reverse negative feedback loops and build increasingly higher levels of self-esteem.

Be Patient. Be Consistent.

It's going to take a bit of time before you really break these patterns. Just as I said on Day 4, you're in the process of consistently pouring new, positive perception over the (concrete) layer protecting your old patterns of thought and behaviour which made up your previous confidence and self-esteem habits.

You need to do the work and you need to do it consistently. Over time, if you do this you can create profound change.

Don't forget the *I Like Myself...* exercise tonight.

DAY 7 – End Of Week Check-In

21 Days Until Reboot

Well done! Congratulate yourself on sticking with the Reboot for the first week. Feel good about yourself – not everyone makes it this far.

The *I Like Myself...* exercise and Reminders should be becoming second nature by now and easier to do. That's great. But don't allow this to make you complacent. Hopefully, by now I've done enough to convince you to power through and continue to be diligent with the exercises.

Maybe you're riding high on day seven. It's also possible you might be feeling challenged at this point. That is a normal part of this process. It's okay. Trust in it and yourself, commit to the whole 28 days and you'll get there.

Take Time To Reflect

Reflect on your journey so far. First of all, have you stuck fully to it? I know you're here reading this, but have you been doing the exercises every single day? Have you been looking at your Reminders page on a daily basis, adding things when you think of them and reviewing them regularly? If you have, bloody awesome!

If you haven't, that's okay – don't beat yourself up. You're still here and you're still engaged. If you've fallen off the wagon, remember it's not about being perfect. There are three weeks still to go. No matter where you are in this process, commit for the remaining 21 days and it will pay off.

Checking In

Open your workbook and remind yourself of the Scale you set

and your Starting Point on page 229. Then turn to the Week 1 Check In on page 230. Draw a line on the scale that you feel represents how you are currently doing. Stay as objective as possible and you can use half increments if you feel that more accurately represents where you are. As long as you stay consistent when using the original scale you can accurately measure your progress over the 28 days.

In the space provided, make a list of all the Notable Improvements you've seen over this past week.

Obviously, I'm hoping you're seeing some positive progress and that your scale has already improved. If it has, staying motivated for the next seven days is unlikely to be a problem. If you're having a bit of a dip, be mindful – this is just a snapshot. It's not necessarily a true reflection of the progress you're making. Maybe Week 1 was challenging for you and Week 2 is when you're going to come good. For some, things don't really kick in until Week 3 or even Week 4. Again, this is why this is a full 28-day programme. As long as you show up for the daily lessons, I'm here to hold your hand every step until the end. The path of creating positive change is rarely linear. There are bound to be some highs and lows on the journey, but if you go the distance you'll end up on top.

If you find yourself struggling at any point on the Reboot, don't forget the extra support available at: www.BiggerBrighterBolder.co.uk/Reboot/Resources. That's where you'll find motivation and support videos, as well as the other resources that accompany this programme.

Well done on completing the first week. I'll see you tomorrow when we kick off Week 2.

DAY 8 – Make <u>YOU</u> A Priority

20 Days Until Reboot

Welcome to Week 2

You're Worth It

Where do you currently come in your list of priorities? Are you the number one priority in your own life, maybe number two, or maybe somewhere near the bottom? If you're like so many, your needs may come below those of your family and friends, below business or work – they might even be below that of the cat or the dog. Where you fall on your priority list could be indicative of your level of self-esteem. For the remainder of this programme, I want you to make yourself a priority.

Making yourself a priority isn't selfish. The more you can improve yourself, the more self-worth you'll have and the greater your self-esteem will be. If you want to be a great wife, husband or partner, high self-esteem is essential. The same goes for parenting and, of course, work or business. Making yourself a priority is better for everyone.

We nurture and prioritise what we love and what's important to us. If we neglect something, it's because we don't value it. If we see that we're neglecting ourselves, we're receiving a clear message that we don't matter. This pushes our self-worth lower, and so on. The opposite is also true. If we see that we're making ourselves a priority, we're receiving a clear message that we matter and our self-worth increases.

Acknowledge Your Desires And Ambitions

Acknowledge your needs, desires and wants. Acknowledge what's important to you. People can find themselves becoming subservient to others for all kinds of reasons. It could be a misguided attempt at being a better partner, parent, friend or carer, for example. But your own desires and ambitions need to be acknowledged.

Beware if those desires include indulging in wine, fish and chips, chocolates, or big binge nights out. These might sound like honouring yourself, but typically these are superficial indulgences designed to temporarily numb us. You get a quick fix from alcohol, sugar, junk food or whatever takes your fancy. They release serotonin and dopamine, but only give a temporary, short-lived high. They're not authentic, positive desires.

We often go through life ignoring ourselves. If we do acknowledge ourselves, it's often in judgemental or critical ways. We highlight what we've done wrong or not well enough. We zero in on our weaknesses and flaws. At the end of the day, when we've often knocked the crap out of our self-esteem, we reach for these indulgences and 'treats' to help us feel a little better.

Big brand advertising companies don't help. They promote the idea that consuming chocolate, ice cream, alcohol or whatever, will make you feel better about yourself and life. If you over-indulge in any of these it could come from a place of low self-esteem. I'm not here to say don't partake in these things, but I want to challenge you to find deeper and more meaningful ways to express your love for yourself.

Do Things That Are Good For YOU

First, stop beating yourself up. Then treat yourself consistently better – acknowledging yourself, what you do well and your successes. Occasionally you might slip up and be mean to yourself. It's okay to mess up. Learn from it and do better next time.

Exercise

Grab a pen and paper and answer these questions.

- What do you love doing that makes you happy?
- What did you used to do that brought joy?
- What are you good at?

Which of the above could you bring more of to your life? Make a specific effort for the next three weeks.

Doing things that make you feel good boosts your self-esteem. So does doing activities that you're skilled at. Of course, you can't always only do these things but indulge yourself as much as you can during the Reboot.

What do you enjoy in your quiet time?

Everyone is different. Some people's quiet time is for meditation, swimming, going to the gym, or just hanging out in a sauna or jacuzzi. For you, perhaps it's walking the dog, a long hot bath, reading a book or just lying down in a quiet room. Make time for these.

Take a few moments to add anything to your list of Reminders that you need to be mindful of. While you're at it, why not open your diary or calendar and make space for a few of these activities right now.

Enjoy Your Own Company

How can you expect to get to know someone if you don't spend time with them?

You need to be happy in your own company. A lot of people spend hardly any waking time on their own. If you want to build a loving relationship with yourself, you need to spend quality time on your own.

We often find ourselves either surrounded by other people or heavily distracted by some form of media. We become disconnected from our self. When we're alone in a peaceful, quiet place, there's no outside influence and we naturally focus inwards. This can be challenging but it's really worth working on getting to know ourselves properly.

I used to detest my own company. I would find excuses to go out and distract myself with other people and I generally cut myself off from my self. Many years later, I can honestly say I'm happiest and most at peace in my own company. It didn't come naturally – I had to work at it. I had to get to know me and look deeper to get past those things I disliked about myself. I had to connect with my true self. I had to find forgiveness for myself. First I learned to stop hating myself. Then I started to like myself. Finally, I loved myself. If I can go on that journey, you can too. This programme is designed to dramatically reduce the length of the time it took me.

CONGRATULATIONS!

By sticking with this programme you've unlocked a hidden bonus.

I have created a wonderful meditation and visualisation to help you fall back in love with yourself and your life.

The Smile visualisation supports the central themes contained within today's lesson. If you enjoy it, listen as often as you can throughout the remainder of the Reboot. You can download or listen to it by following the link for Bonus 1 in the Bonus Material section at:
www.BiggerBrighterBolder.co.uk/Reboot/Resources.

Use the code SMILE to gain access.

If you don't immediately get on with Smile, listen a few more times before writing it off. If after that you still don't enjoy it, it's possible it's just not for you and that's perfectly fine. Including it as part of your Reboot is purely optional.

Don't forget the *I Like Myself...* exercise tonight.

I'll see you tomorrow.

DAY 9 – Beware Perfectionism

19 Days Until Reboot

Perfectionism can lead to stress, anxiety, frustration, a sense of failure, and therefore negatively impact your levels of self-esteem.

Having High Standards Is Good

Having high standards is a good thing. High standards equal high expectations and, as stated on Day 2, this leads to higher personal performance. Whilst this is positive, you always want to beware perfectionism. Perfectionists are driven crazy by the desire for perfection. Many a perfectionist has produced brilliant work, only to disregard it because it didn't match their impossibly high standards.

If you are seeking perfection from yourself on this programme, you're unlikely to make it to the end. Inevitably, you'll make a mistake or fail to complete an exercise, and then you'll likely throw the lot in the bin. Neither of us want that. You need to be compassionate and patient with yourself – especially when you make a mistake or drop the ball.

It Takes One to Know One

This kind of thinking and behaviour is not unfamiliar to me. One of the ways that I used to express myself growing up was with a compulsive desire for perfection. The work I produced had to be perfect. My trainers had to be like new and spotlessly clean. My school books had to be written perfectly – I couldn't make a single mistake. If I did, that was it. I would tear out the page and start all over again. A single scuff on my school shoes and they were ruined. If someone dog-eared a page in a book I was reading, that too was ruined.

Everything had to be perfect. It was hugely anxiety-inducing. If I did one thing wrong, it felt like everything was ruined and spoiled and I can't tell you the number of pieces of work, paintings and all manner of other things that ended up in the bin. Typically, I would destroy them on the way. This behaviour fuelled my already low self-esteem.

Give Yourself Permission Not To Be Perfect

I'm not saying that you're afflicted with perfectionism and the compulsion to keep things perfect to the same degree I was (both impossible tasks), but if you recognise yourself in any of this, learn to take it easy on yourself. Have high standards, by all means, but spare yourself the prison of perfectionism. You can't possibly *do* perfect - no one can. Give yourself permission not to be perfect.

Protect yourself during this process. Once your self-esteem can support it you can start to push a little harder.

Remember

If you self-identify as a perfectionist, maybe you need to remember that you're giving yourself permission not to be perfect or that nothing remains as good as new. Maybe this lesson has brought home some other awareness. Add what you need to remember to the Reminders at the front of your workbook and come back tomorrow.

DAY 10 – People Pleasing Pleases No One

18 Days Until Reboot

Stop Failing To Please Everyone And Start Pleasing Yourself

We should all want to be nice to one another. We should all want to do nice things for other people. The difference between a natural, healthy desire to help others and having negative people-pleasing habits is that the latter is negatively fuelled and self-destructive. I'm not going to say all people pleasing is down to low self-esteem, but low self-esteem can definitely trigger people-pleasing behaviours and a people-pleasing mindset.

People pleasers put everyone else ahead of themselves. They believe that their self-worth is based upon the approval of other people and that if they do enough for others, they will be liked. The irony is that people pleasers often fail to please anyone, least of all themselves. They say yes to too many people and often commit to things they later resent and fail to deliver on.

These people also tend to morph themselves into who other people want or expect them to be. They can lose themselves in an ongoing attempt to be all things to all people. They value what others think they should value and they live out

their life according to other people's ideas of what's right or wrong. They lose sight of what's important to them and what they want to achieve in life. As you can imagine, this plays negatively into their self-esteem, compounding the problem.

Care What People Think, Just Don't Care Too Much

I saw an interview some years ago with the globally acclaimed, inspirational life coach, Tony Robbins. He could be considered a "love him or loathe him" personality and he often receives a lot of criticism and negative judgement. If you don't know of him, Tony is a giant man in every measurable proportion. He's rich, six feet seven inches tall, loud, confident, a force of nature and has worked with some of the most powerful, successful and famous people in the world. He was asked if he cares what people think of him. Paraphrasing, he said that he does care what people think, just not enough to stop being who he's being or doing what he's doing. I loved his response and stole it to use as my own mantra.

With people-pleasing tendencies myself, I have fallen into all the traps mentioned above. I would behave in a way that I believed would appeal to others. I'd contradict my own core values and be, do and say things that I didn't believe in – all in an attempt to make people like me so I that could value myself. But of course, being inauthentic and dishonouring your true nature only makes you dislike yourself more.

In an attempt to counteract this negative expression of my people-pleasing nature, I tried not giving a shit about others. Unsurprisingly, that didn't work for me either. During my own adventures exploring my self-esteem and other issues, I'm pleased to say that I found my balance – my alignment between being a decent human being of value to society and others, and being my true, authentic self. Tony Robbins summed up the accumulation of about ten years of my own personal development in a single sentence. With the utmost of respect, I'd offer my own addendum to his sentiment.

I care deeply what others think about me, just not enough to change who I am, what I'm doing and where I'm going in life!

It's Good To Care

I do care what people think and I try to be mindful of the impact I have on those around me. I want the people close to me to be happy, respect me and like me. I think we should care what people think. However, we shouldn't care enough about what they think to change who it is that we are. We shouldn't change what we're doing and shouldn't compromise on our core values. We should feel empowered to chase our own dreams and goals. None of this should be to the exclusion of others' views, needs or lives. This isn't about being a selfish arsehole, this is about being true to yourself.

Your Authentic Self Is Your Best Self

Being your true self – the version you love and respect – leads to a fulfilling and happy life. It's also the best version to share with others, even those who don't necessarily approve of who that is. This is a tough responsibility to take on, especially if you're a people pleaser. But by being true to yourself, by default you are also being true to those around you.

Tread Carefully

Don't make any drastic changes to your life. Most of the change during this programme occurs on the inside. Of course, these inner changes to your self-esteem will transmute into change in your external environment. The journey of self-discovery is not one you can instantaneously circumnavigate. It will take time – more time than the 28 days you're on this Reboot. Allow yourself the time and space to discover who you are, what's important to you and what you want out of life before making any big decisions.

Start Saying No!

Saying yes to the wrong things leads to you resenting others, breaking commitments, letting others down and lower self-esteem. Conversely, saying no to those things boosts self-worth and self-esteem.

Consider saying no to the following.

- Things you don't want to do.
- Things you can't actually get done.
- Agreeing with someone who you actually disagree with.
- Anything that compromises your own values.

A Cast-Iron <u>NO</u> Creates A Rock-Solid <u>YES</u>

You need a cast-iron no in order to have a strong yes. When you're a people pleaser, you tend to say yes to everyone – but it's not a real yes. You're saying yes because you think they'll like you if you do, or not like you if you don't. It's not an honest yes. You're agreeing under duress – not from them but from yourself.

To have a strong, honest yes, you have to be able to say no. If you can't say no, you can't really say yes. For the people pleaser, saying yes lacks conviction. It's not a yes as much as an avoidance of saying no.

Every time you try to please other people at your own expense, or in violation of your values, you feel worse about yourself. The worse you feel, the lower your self-esteem.

It Can Be Hard To Say No

Start slowly and learn to say no. If you're not used to saying no, don't expect to be perfect at it. There are, in fact, a hundred ways of saying no to people. From the hard, definitive and absolute NO, through to the gentle, compassionate and empathetic no.

Start to exert yourself in the world, pushing back just a little bit. You don't have to be a dick about it. Just don't let your people-pleasing side get you caught in a trap that becomes a negative, self-fulfilling spiral of lower and lower levels of self-esteem.

What do you need to remember about this people-pleasing lesson? Be sure to put whatever you need to in your list of Reminders.

And make sure you're keeping up the momentum with the *I Like Myself...* exercise.

See you tomorrow.

DAY 11 – Tell The Truth And Keep Your Promises

17 Days Until Reboot

Tell The Truth

Whether it's being dishonest, concealing the truth, or blatantly lying through our teeth, lying damages our self-esteem.

Some people lie to protect themselves from being 'found out'. Whilst lying might protect them from the immediate fear of this, it's an expression of their low self-esteem and creates a longer-term problem of disliking themselves. It's another kick in the nether regions for their self-esteem.

Some people lie to cover guilt or shame. However, covering up only draws more of their attention to the guilt or shame, compounding those feelings whilst also suffering the negative effects of their lying. Wham! Down their self-esteem tumbles.

Some lie because they think the truth is too dull, too boring or not good enough. You can fill in the rest, I'm sure, but needless to say it ends with yet another hit to their self-esteem.

And yes, some scumbags lie deliberately to deceive others for their own ill-gotten gains. These guys get what they deserve. The rest of the examples above aren't bad people at all but may have got themselves into a pattern of dishonesty as a protection mechanism for certain vulnerabilities.

There's Strength In Vulnerability

Having vulnerabilities is not a failing or character flaw. It's not a weakness. We all have 'soft spots' and sometimes these can be easy targets for those that would choose to harm us. Maybe you've experienced this in the past and have come to believe that your vulnerabilities must be protected at all costs. Actually, vulnerability is an attractive trait. It's authentic and honest and we can all relate to it. Secretly we are often in awe of those who are able to bravely express their vulnerability. Whilst a minority might turn it against you as a weapon, the rest will connect deeply with it. For those who would use your vulnerability against you, you have to question their self-esteem levels and motives in desiring to bring you down. Be compassionate with them if you can and remember there's real strength in vulnerability, but it takes courage and bravery.

Being Honest With Yourself

Being honest begins with yourself. Until we are comfortable metaphorically standing naked in front of the mirror and observing our true selves, we risk living a lie. A lie we aren't necessarily even in on. Our subconscious conceals the truth and feeds us a lie to protect us from ourselves. For example, blaming others for something we played a part in protects us from taking responsibility. It's much more comfortable when it's someone else's mistake or character flaw rather than our own.

Start the process by being transparent with yourself. You'll need to build self-trust and that takes time. Your subconscious needs to feel safe telling you truths and letting you in on its little secrets. If you find out something negative or that you don't like about yourself, don't punish yourself for it. If you ask a child to tell the truth about whether they stole the last sweet and, when they tell you they did, you ground them and ban sweets for life, don't expect them to tell you the truth ever again. The same goes for you. It must be safe for you to be honest with yourself. How can you possibly begin to be honest with others until that's the case?

The Truth Will Set You Free

Once you have greater transparency and honesty within yourself and you feel safe in that space, you will naturally start to feel stronger and take that out into the world around you. When you can live safely and freely as your authentic, honest self, you are free – free from the judgement of others. You are who you are and you do what you do, unapologetic and transparent. If someone doesn't like that, it says nothing about you and everything about them. The people who you will attract in your life will be those who love and respect you for who you truly are. The more you can be honest and vulnerable without fear, the more your self-esteem will grow.

Start Slowly

As with everything in this programme, go at your own pace and only do what you're comfortable doing. Start being a little more honest with yourself and, if up to it, honest with the world. The more you can be truthful and honest with yourself and other people, the better you're going to feel about yourself. It's a sure-fire way to build your self-esteem. But be cautious. Going at it too aggressively could be counterproductive at this stage and backfire.

Keep Your Promises

When you say you're going to do something, do it. If you've committed to something or someone, follow through. If you can't deliver, don't make the promise. Empty promises that you don't stick to damage your self-esteem and possibly your relationships with anyone else involved.

Yesterday I talked about saying no when you're not committed or you don't want to do something. That's being honest and truthful. If you say yes to someone when you really mean no, you're lying. If you're lying to them, you're potentially spiralling down into lower levels of self-esteem.

Your truthfulness doesn't have to be brutal or hurtful. It can be sympathetic, compassionate and understanding. Honour yourself by giving yourself the option of not promising or committing to something you don't want to do. If you still choose to make a promise, make sure you're doing it for all the right reasons and then follow through. Don't break those promises.

Have an awesome day and come back tomorrow.

DAY 12 – Dare To Love Yourself

16 Days Until Reboot

Please make sure you're keeping up the momentum with the *I Like Myself...* process. It should be becoming second nature by now. Don't forget to read through your Reminders – these are starting to take root so don't let up.

Loving Yourself Can Be Challenging

The reason you've been doing the daily *I Like Myself...* exercise is to build the habit of self-acknowledgement, uncovering what you like about yourself with a view to loving yourself as a whole.

Loving yourself can be incredibly challenging. But until you love yourself fully, life simply will not deliver the quality of experience it otherwise could. That doesn't mean you have to approve of everything you do. Imagine you're the perfect parent. If your child misbehaves, you may not approve of that behaviour but you still love them unconditionally for everything that they are.

Many of us never learned the ability to experience that unconditional love for ourselves. Others unlearned it. The love you need for yourself has to be nurtured and that's at the core of what you're doing throughout this entire Reboot. But I get it – this can be confronting.

It's possible you fear loving yourself in case you lose the drive to fix what you see as being wrong with you. For example, if someone dislikes their body because it's overweight and out of shape, they might find the idea of loving their body an impossible notion. How can they love something that isn't how they want it to be? Also, if they loved it, would they still have the motivation to change it? It's completely natural to think this way.

The experience of disliking or hating something is evolution's way of generating a response in us to either change it or get rid of it. If we dislike a person, we're subconsciously being directed to keep our distance or ditch them altogether. If we translate that experience to our car, for example, we're being manipulated into replacing it. It's a response to a perception that the object of the dislike or hate isn't enough or isn't good for us. We're judging the object based on a concept or idea of what is or isn't good enough - it's very subjective.

What if the object of the dislike or hate is our self? We become both the focus of and the one experiencing that dislike.

How Is Disliking Yourself Working Out For You?

We automatically don't take care of the things we dislike. An old mobile phone we've fallen out of love with gets tossed to the bottom of a drawer with bunches of keys and old coins when once it was our pride and joy. The old car with a few dings and dents gets no love or attention compared to when it was brand new, loved and handwashed and polished every Sunday. We don't lift a finger for the person we dislike but go to the ends of the earth for the one we love. If we hate ourselves, we disrespect ourselves and treat ourselves badly. If we love ourselves, we nurture, protect and take care of ourselves. Therefore, whilst hating ourselves might put more pressure on us to create change, we are, in fact, less likely to make that change happen.

If you dislike or even hate yourself, how has that worked out for you? Have you changed the parts you dislike the most? If you're like most people, you haven't – you've just kept on disliking yourself. Too many people put off loving themselves until they feel worthy of love but never achieve that goal because their disliking of themselves gets in the way. Disliking ourselves lowers self-esteem and lower self-esteem leads to disliking ourselves even more. You are unlikely to create the change you seek from a place of low self-esteem.

We Take Care Of The Things We Love

We treat the things we love with respect and care. We protect them and nurture them and the same goes for ourselves. For example, if we love and are positively connected to our bodies we tend to treat them well. We nourish them with good, nutritious food, exercise and plenty of sleep. If we hate or are disconnected from our bodies, we neglect and abuse them. Therefore we need to love our bodies into the change we want to see.

If your body is a focus of your self-dislike, think of it this way. Your body is an incredible thing. It tirelessly works to give you the best it's got. It gives you your experience of this life. It constantly protects you from illness and heals itself when injured. It takes all the abuse you give it and still it keeps going. People abuse themselves to extreme levels and yet their bodies continue to serve them the best they can. Love your body. It deserves to be loved. It's an incredible thing that will serve you to the best of its ability for as long as it possibly can. It never gives up on you – you should never give up on it. Try loving it for its awesomeness rather than disliking it for its flaws (as you see them).

Try this new perspective for yourself. Your issue might not be your body, it could be anything to do with your physical, emotional or mental self. It might be your ability or inability to do something. Whatever it is, stop hating you for who you're not and start loving you for who you are. When you love yourself, you automatically start treating yourself better and that's how you create positive change in yourself, your life and of course your self-esteem.

No One Is Born Hating Themselves

Who the hell told you what you should or shouldn't be like, anyway? No newborn has self-esteem issues. No baby hates themselves and there are no babies with a negative self-image. We are not born this way. Whilst our evolution gave us the power to dislike and hate things, we learnt how to focus that hate on ourselves. Maybe for you it stems from an experience when you were younger. Maybe it was negative lessons you learned from the media, movies, popstars or the covers of magazines. Maybe something was said directly to you in your past, or you overheard criticism about someone else and took that on as your own.

We often receive the message, directly or indirectly, that we are not good enough. But we're being lied to. Imagine the perfect baby you once were with all your unlimited potential. That's still in you, desiring nothing more than to be loved for simply being. Don't put off loving yourself until you're 'good enough', based on flawed concepts of what good enough is or isn't. Give yourself the love you deserve, today.

Change Or Don't Change – You Choose

Ignore the rules you might have picked up along the journey of life and make any changes you desire to make for the right reasons. Don't lose weight so you can be loved, desirable, good enough or worthy. Lose weight because you want to lose weight for you. Lose weight because you want to extend and improve the quality of your life. Lose weight to move better and keep ill-health at bay. Or don't. There are no rules about what you should or shouldn't do. Just actions and consequences. Choose to change or choose not to. But regardless of whether you do or don't, never compromise on loving yourself. The same goes for any and all aspects of you and your life.

Boosting Self-Esteem

While there are no rules for what you should change about yourself, creating positive change does boost your self-esteem. The greater your self-esteem, the more objective you can be about yourself and the more empowered you are to create the change you wish to see, without resorting to disliking yourself.

Loving yourself will raise your self-esteem and raising your self-esteem will mean you love yourself more. The more you love yourself, the better you'll feel, the more confident you'll be and the more fully and boldly you'll present yourself to the world around you.

Change The Things You Can
Love The Things You Can't

Whilst it's possible to alter or change many things about ourselves, there might be things you can't do anything about. Maybe it's a physical attribute, such us height, or perhaps a mental or physical disability. Change what you want to and what you can but love everything, regardless. Love it all.

Success and happiness are built on self-esteem. Beating yourself up over aspects of who you are will limit your ability to create the change you want. I know it can be scary and if you are being challenged by this, trust me, you're not the only one. I've gone through this process myself and it can be scary and emotional. But the relationship with oneself can be the most rewarding relationship of all.

Take care and love yourself. You are worthy of it.

DAY 13 – Guilt-Free Living

15 Days Until Reboot

The subject of guilt can be a challenging one for many people. Guilt can be both an expression of low self-esteem and, at the same time, cause low self-esteem. Guilt damages people's lives.

What Is Guilt?

If we understand what guilt is and why we have it, we can start to let go of it. And that's the objective of today's lesson. In my introduction to this book, I talked about what I call Mindset Mechanics. This is my model for explaining the complex relationship between our mindset, thoughts, feelings and behaviours, and it includes guilt.

We all recognise guilt in ourselves from time to time, maybe in small ways if we tell a little white lie or forget someone's birthday. This form of guilt by itself is unlikely to cause us any major problems. We recognise that it's there because we let someone down or did something a bit 'naughty'. It's another of those pesky evolutionary manipulations designed to keep us safe but today it often gets in the way of opportunity.

Back In The Beginning

Back in our species' distant past, long before we were able to use fine judgement to make lucid and cognitive decisions, all we had were unconscious emotional manipulations. We needed mechanisms to decipher safe and unsafe behaviour. In our most primitive past, this was as simple as which direction of travel was more favourable than another. As we evolved and started to form groups and tribes, life got more complicated and we needed more complex mechanisms for safety.

Tribal Living

Tribal living was a massive step forward in our evolution. We collaborated, shared labour and protected each other. If we were injured the tribe would take care of us. This evolution makes a lot of sense. If the tribe supported us when we needed it we would be a positive contributor to the tribe in the future. If we shared food and resources we all fared much better, and if we put our life on the line for the tribe, it did the same for us. We thrive better in numbers but that degree of collaborative living requires some serious policing.

The balancing act of maintaining a harmonious collective would not be possible with the more primitive responses of self-interest that came from our previous existence as solitary animals. If one member didn't pull their weight, the tribe was out of balance. If one member couldn't be trusted, the entire tribe would be weakened. Guilt was of primary importance in maintaining this fragile balance of trust and fairness.

If someone did something that harmed the tribe, the tribe would harm them back. Retribution might have been as severe as death or, if the transgression didn't require such a harsh sentence, the perpetrator might have been alienated from the tribe. This was a far harsher sentence than it might first appear. If you didn't have the security of the tribe, you were far less safe.

Guilt – Judge, Jury And Executioner

Guilt protected us from ourselves and the tribe from us. If our ancient ancestors did something that went against the best interest of the tribe, everyone was the worse for it. If they were caught, as I said, they would face severe punishment. If they got away with it, what would stop them doing it again? Eventually they'd be caught and punished. In the meantime, the tribe was weakened by their behaviour. Could you imagine a tribe full of individuals all trying to get one over on the rest? They'd be better off alone. Instead, their fear of being caught would deter them from doing it in the first place and, if that failed to stop them, guilt would kick in after.

Guilt serves multiple aims. Firstly, predicting future guilt serves to prevent acting in ways that violate collaborative living. Secondly, feeling guilt during a transgression stops the individual from completing the act. Thirdly, it punishes the individual without anyone else having to find out. Guilt is an uncomfortable experience. The pain of guilt after a transgression will often stop repeat offences. Fourthly, it manipulates a powerful urge to make things right. In short, guilt stops us, punishes us and prevents repeat offending. Lastly, should we be found out, by signalling our guilt we reassure the tribe that we have learned our lesson, allowing them to rebuild their trust in us.

Don't Sit In Guilt

It's possible to sit in guilt for prolonged periods in the unconscious belief that somehow you are serving a sentence for a previous wrongdoing. Maybe you feel that somehow you can't trust yourself not to transgress in the same way again, or that there is something you need to put right. There is no need for prolonged guilt. You can either learn your lesson so you don't do it again or resolve the situation and move on. Either way, it has served its purpose. Let it go. If you feel you should make things right but for whatever reason you can't, let it go just the same.

Guilt Won't Make You A Better Person

When my twin daughters were very young, I split from their mother. I felt so much guilt. I felt like the worst dad ever. Despite many years of personal development, I didn't release any of that guilt. Up until the girls were ten years old I was unconsciously using guilt to fuel me to be a 'good dad'. I also unconsciously believed there was a punishment I needed to serve for not having stayed with them.

The realisation that I'd been subconsciously holding onto guilt in an attempt to positively steer me gave me the awareness that I didn't need it anymore. I realised I was and always had been a great dad. Acknowledging this allowed me to release the guilt. I simply didn't need it to make me a good dad – I already was one. Furthermore, I didn't need punishing. I hadn't done anything wrong.

Unburdening myself of guilt raised my self-esteem, freed me from my prison sentence and made me an all-round better person. It also made me a better dad.

Accept this for yourself. The guilt you're holding onto is limiting your level of self-esteem and damaging your life. You almost certainly don't need it. You're a good person. No doubt, like the best of us, you've not been perfect and there are things you'd do differently now. If so, you've learned your lessons and no longer need the guilt.

Forgiveness Heals Guilt

Forgiving others heals resentment. Forgiving yourself heals guilt and shame. We often crave forgiveness from those we hurt so we can let go of our guilt. Whilst I encourage you to make things right with those you wrong, it's not needed to release you from guilt. It's not always possible to make things right. Sometimes the party we've wronged isn't willing or able to forgive us. Sometimes they're no longer in our life. Forgiving yourself will set you free from your guilt.

Whilst we're on the subject of forgiveness, consider forgiving those who have wronged you. Holding onto resentment is meant to protect us from the person being able to hurt us again. If they are no longer in our lives, we don't need protecting from them. Let any resentment go. If they are in our lives and regret what they've done, they've learned their lesson and we no longer need protecting from them. Resentment is a negative experience, just like guilt. Let go of your resentment and release them from their own guilt. Even if those who have wronged you show no remorse, forgive them – you will be better for it.

Exercise

To relieve yourself of your guilt, follow this process.

- What guilt or shame are you holding onto?
- Did you do anything wrong? If not, let it go.
- If you did do something wrong, can you make it right? If you can, do so.
- If you can't make it right, would you do it again? If no, let it go.
- If you think you would potentially do it again, look at why that might be. What needs to change for you to be able to trust yourself in the future? Make that happen.

Set Yourself Free

You cannot change the past. You can't undo what's already

done. But you can learn from your mistakes so that you can be a better person moving forward. If you get trapped in guilt, you limit your ability to apply that better self in service of your own goals and to the betterment of those around you.

Much of the guilt you feel is unrelated to any specific wrong you've committed. Other aspects of your guilt are related to previous wrongdoings. Let the former go and forgive and heal the latter.

It's time.

DAY 14 – Checking In

Welcome to Day 14 of The 28-Day Self-Esteem Reboot. You've made it to the half-way mark!

Today is a day of reflection.

Take some time to reflect on how far you've already come on this journey. Acknowledge any bigger, more significant changes you've felt, seen or created. Also, acknowledge any smaller but still significant gains you've made.

Checking In

Open your workbook and remind yourself of the Scale you set and your Starting Point on page 229. Also, recap where you were this time last week on page 230. On the same page, complete the Check In for Week 2. Draw a line on the scale that you feel represents how you are currently doing. Stay as objective as possible and you can use half increments if you feel you need that level of accuracy. As long as you stay

consistent when using the scale you'll be accurately measuring your progress over the 28 days.

In the space provided, make a list of all the Notable Improvements you've made this past week.

Once again, if you've taken a little bit of a dip this week, or specifically today, it's okay. You're only halfway through the programme – there's plenty of time to go. Don't forget, the support videos are there to help you at any point if you find you're struggling on your journey. They can be viewed along with all the other supporting resources at: www.BiggerBrighterBolder.co.uk/Reboot/Resources. How have you been getting on with the bonus Smile meditation? Remember you can download or listen to it by visiting www.BiggerBrighterBolder.co.uk/Reboot/Smile.

If you're seeing any kind of positive change it'll be clear that this is working and you should feel inspired to continue. If the changes are small or hard to find it will be more difficult. It's important to acknowledge any small improvement, but if you really can't find any you will need to rely on your commitment to the process and trust that it is working. The process is taking effect, albeit maybe invisibly under the bonnet. You've come a long way already. Make sure you finish what you've started.

Be mindful of the lesson on Day 4 – you're slowly switching from red to blue fuel in your system. For some, progress is fast at the beginning, while for others progress is slower but accelerates later in the process.

Don't Let Up

If you've seen great improvements and find the process is getting easy for you, don't cut corners or think you're done. There's much more still to glean from this programme and the process. Continue to follow the *I Like Myself...* exercises to the letter and continually check in with your Reminders. Also, fully participate in the exercises that follow in the second half of the Reboot.

In Some Ways, We're Still Just Getting Started

The Self-Esteem Reboot is a programme of two halves and from tomorrow we start to turn up the heat a little. I know you're up for it.

Enjoy your day and I'll see you then.

DAY 15 – Stepping It Up A Gear

13 Days Until Reboot

You've now completed fourteen days of the *I Like Myself...* exercise, fourteen days of lessons and fourteen days of focussing on yourself and your self-esteem. You've been looking at the list of what it is you need to remember every day and hopefully you're becoming increasingly comfortable with the whole process.

I hope that you're starting to see positive shifts in your confidence and self-esteem. You may even have started to see changes to your thought patterns, perceptions and behaviour. But as I said yesterday, it's also okay if you haven't. You still have two weeks to go and everyone responds differently to the process. You are on your own journey, tackling your specific issues at your pace, and that's exactly how it should be.

Setting Up The Second Half

As stated at the outset, this is a programme of two halves and from today you're going to make one very powerful shift in your daily practices. However, you're still going to continue with the *I Like Myself...* exercise and adding to your list of Reminders. I know you're becoming very familiar with these practices and it would be easy to start shortcutting the process. Please don't.

The stepped approach to uncovering the *I Like Myself...* statement has been specifically designed to uncover the aspects of yourself that are bringing the greatest benefit to your quality of life, and for you to own them. This makes them much more powerful than the hollow gesture of repeating vapid affirmations to yourself.

The first half of this programme was about gaining awareness. The big shift over the next two weeks is deliberately and proactively taking action that aligns with the personality traits that you most like about yourself.

Identifying The Best Of The Best Of You

You've already collected pages of *I Like Myself...* statements over the past two weeks – well done. Go through them now and identify repeated patterns. You might find repetition in the statements themselves or perhaps in the highlights or the part you played. Don't get hung up on specific wording – you're looking for general repeating themes. These patterns say a lot about certain aspects of yourself that are contributing to the best of who you are.

Turn to the Repeated Themes page in your workbook on page 198 and, referencing all your *I Like Myself...* statements, list anything that jumps out at you. This is an important part of setting up the remainder of the programme, so do it now and read on once you've done that.

Welcome Back

If you haven't done the Repeated Themes exercise, do it now and then read on.

What did you uncover? It's possible that a few themes and repeated patterns were immediately visible to you. Maybe you had to work a little harder to find the commonalities. Is there one particular theme or pattern that really stands out? It might stand out because it shows itself more prolifically in the list, or perhaps it's a repeated pattern that you are most drawn to. Once you've identified your primary stand-out theme, is there a second? Maybe a third? These might be character traits, actions or behaviours. You won't want to focus on any more than three. Once you've identified these, add them to the Deliberate Action List on page 199.

Next, think of ways and opportunities to deliberately act in accordance with that list. This might include things you do, places you go, people you see frequently, or anything specific coming up in your diary. You're not committing to anything at this stage, just identifying opportunities. Add these to your Deliberate Action List.

If you remind yourself who you want to be and what it is you want to do at the beginning of each day, you're priming your subconscious to seek out these opportunities. You might find it a little difficult to start with, but as the days progress you'll start finding that your subconscious habitually starts looking for them. To aid this process, add what's relevant to your list of Reminders so that you get your daily prompt. Also consider where else you could leave reminders for yourself so that you will see them throughout the day.

I Double Dare You

For the next 14 days (starting today if there's still time), proactively look for opportunities to deliberately be that person or do those things. Taking the data you've been collecting over the last 14 days, it's time to start being the person you most like being.

Every day from now on you'll be looking for opportunities to live, be and do deliberately in alignment with those themes that you most like about yourself. You'll continue with the *I Like Myself...* exercises and those may or may not reflect these themes, but continue with them regardless. As you get more data over the next seven to fourteen days, you may find that other themes start to come forward. If at any point you feel there's another theme that you want to add to your Deliberate Action List, go for it. If something comes forward which you think is more important than what you're currently doing, feel free to swap them out.

Being who you like being, and behaving in ways that align with that, should be a rewarding experience. But you might find it challenging as well, especially if others around you aren't totally on board with this version of you. Be bold and brave and be the person you need to be for yourself. I dare you to step up to this challenge for the next 14 days.

Aligning Yourself

When you behave or take action that's out of alignment with what you like about yourself, that will negatively impact your self-esteem. When you begin to take deliberate action towards being the person you most like being, that's going to boost your self-esteem. Your raised self-esteem will express itself as improved confidence. You will also start to create results that align with this best version of yourself. This is where you will begin to see things really take shape. Commit to the next 14 days and dig in.

See you tomorrow.

DAY 16 – Aligning Your Actions

12 Days Until Reboot

Yesterday we finished by talking about aligning your actions with the version of yourself you want to be. This is the main focus of the second half of this programme – deliberately aligning yourself with those thoughts, feelings, actions and behaviours that make you feel increasingly better about yourself and which are also aligned with creating the outcomes and success that you want.

Who Are You?

Who you are today is an amalgamation of the lessons and experiences you have received since birth. These moulded you into who you should be, what you should think, and how you should act, interact with and react to the world around you. As you grew up, social pressures, experiences and circumstances added to the mix. Even to this day, all the information in your field of experience forms the data your subconscious references when deciding on how best you should act and react to life's situations.

How you act and react gets you specific results. If these results are not what you want for yourself, you need to change your behaviours. Your behaviours are a reaction to your thoughts and feelings, so these need to change as well. Bottom line – you need to be different in order to do different, so that you can get different results.

Your Life Fits You Perfectly

Your life is a result of what you've done and who you've been until this point in time. The reason you might feel uncomfortable in your life is that you've potentially created a version of yourself that deep down doesn't align with who you really are and therefore have moulded a life that doesn't fit your true self. The more you feel the restrictions of the life you've created, the harder it can seem to authentically exert yourself in it. Also, those around you treat you as the version of the person they've grown used to, making it even more challenging.

It's possible that you've been playing your current role for so long that you believe yourself to be that person. This is what we are looking at today – changing your perception of yourself.

Someone's Always Watching

Hopefully you're starting to get comfortable with the connection between the subconscious and its manipulation of who you are and what you do. It's based on all of your life's experiences. Your subconscious aligns your behaviours with your identity and is continually building upon its reference point of who you are based on what it witnesses you doing, who you are being and how others interact with you. It's

solidifying your identity and creating your self-image. It's a self-fulfilling feedback loop that reinforces your current identity and self-image. This process is happening unconsciously but, over time and with enough persistence and consistency, you can consciously and intentionally change who you are, based on your desired self-image. With the second half of this programme we are beginning that process.

Change Who You Think You Are

If you met someone new for the first time, they would base their opinion of who you are on what they witnessed in the form of your behaviours and interaction. If you wanted to portray yourself differently you would demonstrate different behaviours. Why would they think you were anything but this version of you? However, when someone already has a strong view of who you are it is much harder to convince them that you're anything different. The same goes for convincing yourself.

The notion of 'fake it till you make it' – whilst true to some degree when meeting a new person – doesn't hold up with people we know well, and no one knows us better than ourselves. We know when we're trying to bullshit ourselves. It's easier creating deep-rooted self-transformation when we first find existing evidence of that which we wish to become.

Once we see the possibility of being who we want to be, we need to align ourselves with our new self-concept. We're not denying who we have been, we're just focussing on who we're becoming. The more we hold our focus on our new identity, the easier it is to align our new behaviours. The more our subconscious sees who we are becoming, the more it recognises us as that person. It takes time, but if we consistently focus on who we are becoming, our actions and behaviours, and therefore our results, will subconsciously align.

Show Yourself Who You Really Are

Before your subconscious starts to do the heavy lifting for you, you will need to do the work yourself. Be intentional and deliberate in choosing to align your behaviours and actions with those core values that ultimately make you feel good about yourself. This is what the second half of the Reboot is about – taking deliberate action that aligns with what you've already discovered you like about yourself.

I want you to start showing yourself the person you really are and the person you're becoming and increasingly choosing to be. Your subconscious will learn from that and start to take on the new identity. I know it can be difficult to do something that initially may feel uncomfortable but, through the feedback process described above, this gets easier with time.

It's Not A Race

The more assertive and consistent you are – thinking, doing and being in alignment with your chosen identity – the quicker you will become that person. However, regardless of how hard you go at it, this will take time. Pace yourself to go the distance. Much better to go to the gym, start training at a comfortable level and build from there, than to jump straight in and do three-hour sessions. The former you can maintain – the latter will burn you out. But go too slow and you'll get frustrated and possibly quit. There's an important balance to strike here.

If you're comfortable sharing this journey with those close to you it can be powerful to get their buy-in and support. When they know what you're trying to achieve they will be more supportive, less critical and less confused by what's going on for you.

If this is challenging for you because you know there are people close to you who might not support you becoming who you choose to be for yourself, start on the inside work first. Adapt your thinking and perception of yourself. Start to design who you want to be. Change your actions and behaviours slowly and begin with the environments in which you feel safest to do so – see Day 5 if you've forgotten what they are.

This will get the ball rolling and build the confidence and self-esteem needed to bring this to all areas of your life.

Start finding ways to show yourself who you choose to be and come back tomorrow.

DAY 17 – A Lesson In Chemistry

11 Days Until Reboot

Today I have a short
chemistry lesson for you.
Don't yawn. Don't fall
asleep. This is chemistry
you'll seriously want to
understand.

Serotonin

If you or someone you
know has ever suffered
with depression, you
may already know about
serotonin and its links to your mood. However, what you may
not know is that serotonin is also what regulates your self-
esteem. When we have lower levels of serotonin, we have
lower levels of self-esteem. When we have high levels of
serotonin, we have high levels of self-esteem.

The aim of this Reboot is to have consistently high levels of
self-esteem. So one of the ways we can ensure that is by
making sure we consistently have high levels of serotonin.

Don't Run To The Doc Just Yet

This isn't a call for you to go to your doctor and ask for
serotonin or antidepressants. There are simple actions you can
take to maintain and boost your levels of serotonin.

Feedback from those around you can increase or decrease
your serotonin levels. If you keep putting yourself in the
proximity of critical or negative feedback the levels in your

bloodstream decrease, thereby reducing your self-esteem. When you put yourself in the proximity of positive feedback, the opposite occurs.

This is why I gave you permission to protect yourself back on Day 3. Protect yourself from criticism and surround yourself with those who positively reflect who you are.

Get On Your Cycle

Serotonin fires in cycles. When you're sitting around, not doing anything, it fires at about three cycles per second. When you get up and start moving it goes up to five cycles per second. In simple terms, when you're sitting at your desk or lazing around like a couch potato, you're not getting the same serotonin hit as you would be if you were being more active.

When you do heavy exercise it massively boosts your serotonin levels. A study suggests that taking up running could be as beneficial for relieving depression as taking antidepressants. Disclaimer: If you're on antidepressants, this is not to say you should stop taking them. Always seek professional advice.

If you are more active, your serotonin levels go up as does your self-esteem. In our modern life, it's not uncommon to sit at a desk or in a chair for most of the day, followed by an evening of lazing on the couch. This is unhealthy for us on all levels, and for the purposes of this process it's not good for our mood (serotonin levels) or self-esteem either.

In your mission to raise and maintain your self-esteem, sitting on your arse directly opposes this ambition. You don't need to be doing extreme exercise to get the benefit from moving. Going for a walk or jumping on an exercise bike in front of the TV will do the job.

The More You Move The Better

Look for opportunities to move more. Having a good baseline of activity is a great way to start. Get up and move around regularly. Remember, just getting up and walking around takes your serotonin from three to five cycles per second. Taking regular, more intense exercise boosts it further still. I must add a caveat here and say, obviously, you should not suddenly undertake a massive new exercise regime without consulting an appropriate professional. What I can suggest is to stop sitting around and start moving more. Get more active and boost your self-esteem. It's a simple thing that you can do now. Just stand up and move around instead of sitting down all day. Maybe make a commitment to do your phone calls as you wander around the office, house or garden, instead of taking them at your desk, and to be more mindful when sitting for long periods.

The Hardest Part Of The Run
Is Getting Your Trainers On

If you're not an active person or are struggling with your mood, you are unlikely to be motivated to start jumping around. But that's exactly what you need to do. Getting started is always the hardest step. We have a limited supply of willpower and running on willpower alone means you'll never go the distance. Luckily, nature has a solution. You only need willpower to get you moving. From there, momentum takes over.

Don't try and run five miles purely on willpower. Use willpower to get your trainers on and get you started. Whether it's going for a walk, swim, run, ride, or to the gym, use your willpower to get you across the start line. Once you're moving, momentum will kick in.

Move In Ways That Make You Happy And Maybe Get A Dog

That said, if you hate running don't take up running. If you hate the gym don't bother with a membership. Anything you do that moves your body will be beneficial to your health, your mood and your self-esteem. So do things you enjoy doing. A survey showed that dog owners typically get more exercise than gym members and, with the proven benefit pets have on mental and emotional health, maybe this is the perfect time to consider that four-legged, self-esteem-boosting, furry friend you always wanted. And, there's nothing like a dog for teaching you how special you are.

Exercise

Grab a pen and make a list of all the ways you could move more. From working standing up, walking the dog, gardening or DIY projects, to your favourite cardio or workout routines – maybe you've always fancied rock climbing, horse riding or renovating an old table – if it keeps you moving, it's all good. If it moves you it boosts your serotonin and your self-esteem.

Easy-peasy!

Add anything you want to remember to your list of Reminders and keep up the *I Like Myself...* routine.

DAY 18 – Create Yourself Based On Your Own Design

10 Days Until Reboot

Don't forget to keep referencing your Reminders each morning. Also, make sure you are deliberately being and doing in alignment with your Deliberate Action List. If you've fallen off the wagon with any of the excercises, use today to jump back on.

Once you start to work out who you need to be for you and what you want out of life, you can start to carve that out for yourself. Be mindful to stay focused on who you want to be and not who you believe you should be. Becoming the person someone else thinks you should be is a negative expression of people pleasing and only ends in low self-esteem.

We are different things to different people and we all wear different hats in life – the business hat, the parent hat, the performer, the leader or the student. The problem isn't having multiple hats. The issue comes if we hide our true self behind a mask and pretend to be something that we're not.

No One Was Working To A Plan

Imagine giving ten people a lump of clay and asking them

to sculpt a human being together without collaborating. One person works on a leg while someone else is working on another leg. Meanwhile, a third person is working on yet another leg. They're not working as a team and no one is looking at the whole. They're independently building what they think a human being should be based on their own experience and prejudices. Someone might be shaping a sturdy, muscular arm, while the other arm is taking on a slimmer form. The end result is a deformed representation of a human being, based on the individual perspective of each sculptor acting independently from the others.

We have each had our own collection of sculptors shaping us throughout our lives – our parents, teachers, friends and society have all played their part in making us who we are today. But no one held the overall plan. Influential people in our lives went about shaping us based on their own ideals – a chaotic more than a collaborative approach. The result is there for you to see in yourself – contradictory ideas that run through your mind and behaviours which counteract your chosen wants and desires. But just because you had very little say in this process, doesn't mean it's all bad. There is much in you that is perfect as it is, moulded together with other aspects that you wouldn't choose for yourself. There's no need to discard all that you are to start again. That's as unnecessary as it is impossible.

Get The Modelling Tools Out

It's time to take out the modelling tools to begin sculpting the person you want to be out of the raw materials you've been given in life. No matter how hard it can be to see, you have the basic essentials needed to start recreating yourself based on your own design.

Exercise

To help you, answer these questions about who you want to be:

- How do you want to think?
- How do you want to feel?
- How do you want to act?
- What is it you want to create in life?
- Ultimately, what's the life you want to live?

Make a note of the most important answers in your Reminders. These will give you a destination – a place to aim for. If you take the consistent action that bridges the gap from where you are to those outcomes, you will get there. Shaping your thought patterns, personality and identity is the same as shaping your body. Hold a clear vision of what you want to achieve and work on it consistently over time.

You can change almost anything – you just can't change everything right now. Pick an area you want to improve and work on that. If you want to be courageous, challenge yourself a little every day. If you want to stop the negative self-talk in your head, catch those thoughts as they happen and replace them with something more supportive. If you want to be more organised, work on it little by little.

Create yourself based on your own design.

See you tomorrow.

DAY 19 – Stick To Your Agenda

9 Days Until Reboot.

Know Where You're Going

If you're not on your agenda, the chances are you're on someone else's. Throughout this programme I've drawn your attention to your agenda. Saying no, for example, protects you from being dragged onto someone else's agenda which doesn't serve or align with you. But you want to go one step further.

You first need to know where you're heading. You'll want to create a vision for your life and who you wish to become. You'll want to set goals and targets that get you there. You'll also want to create a plan and devise the right tactics to bridge the gap between where you are and where you want to be. Setting out your agenda in this way is a proven strategy for accomplishment and living a fulfilling life. It's beyond the remit of this programme to go into detail about how to do this but, for now, start with the end in mind.

Dare To Dream

Having a dream gives you hope. It gives your life direction. A dream inspires you to step up to life, work hard and face challenges head on. In short, a dream gives you something to live for – something that's bigger than you. We touched on this at the end of yesterday's lesson – let's take it further.

Exercise

Grab a pen and ask yourself the following questions.

If you dared to dream:

- What would that dream look like?
- Where would you be living?
- What would you be doing?
- Who would be with you?
- How would you feel?
- How would you act and behave?
- If you looked in a mirror, what would you see?

Answering these questions starts to formulate your vision for you and your life. As your self-esteem and confidence grow your dream will start to feel more achievable. The more you focus on the dream, the more you'll tangibly connect with it. The bigger the dream, the longer it will take to achieve and, of course, the harder you'll need to work.

Corridor Visualisation

If you haven't listened to the Corridor Visualisation in a while, give it another go, it will help. Goto:
www.BiggerBrighterBolder.co.uk/Reboot/Resources

Set Goals

Once you know where you're heading you'll need to stay on track. Allowing yourself to be pulled from agenda to agenda will derail your journey to your dreams. Having a cast-iron agenda of your own is the surest way of getting on track with your own life. This isn't to say you won't do things for others, it just means you'll be mindful when you do.

Setting goals and achieving them boosts confidence and self-esteem – doubly so if you take the time to enjoy your wins, both big and small. At the beginning of this programme, I said not to set yourself up for failure. And this is still true. However, depending on how you are feeling now you can choose whether to set yourself some small, short-term goals and targets. If you're not feeling it quite yet, that's fine. Remember this lesson and come back to it when you are.

Start Small

If you do decide to set yourself some goals and targets, start small. Set yourself up for success. The bigger the goal and the more challenging it is and the harder you have to work to achieve it, the more your confidence, self-esteem and satisfaction will grow. However, the chances of failure also increase. With failure can come a knock to your self-esteem and confidence, especially if those aren't solid beforehand. Better to develop your confidence with goal setting and achievement and build slowly to increasingly challenging objectives.

You want to align any small goals you set yourself with your bigger, long-term dreams. For example, if you want to build a bigger business or better career, set small goals that take you in this direction. Taking small steps forward will soon build momentum.

Your Agenda Is Important

What you want matters. Who you wish to become matters. Whether it's a simple task, a goal or your lifelong ambition, what you want to do and create in this world is important.

Add anything you need to your list of Reminders and keep up with the daily exercises and routines.

Congratulations!

By sticking with the programme, you have unlocked bonus content.

Creating a visual representation of the best version of yourself and life can be far more powerful than a shopping list. I've recorded a video to assist you in how you might want to go about this. The result will be an empowering and inspiring work of art that you can look at each and every day. You may even be so inspired by your creation that you'll display it with pride. Follow the link for Bonus 2 in the Bonus Material section at: www.BiggerBrighterBolder.co.uk/Reboot/Resources.

Use the code BESTLIFE to gain access.

Day 20 – It's None Of Your Business What Other People Think

It's none of your business what people think about you. Any issues people may have with you belong to them. Let them have them. You cannot control what people think and feel about you. On the Reboot we are far more interested in what you think and feel about yourself. When it comes to our self-esteem, that's all that matters. But when positive feedback can make us feel good and negative opinions can seemingly destroy us, it can be hard to compute that other people's opinions are unimportant.

Take Back Your Power

We need to take back the power we so freely give to others. If we are hurt by someone's negative opinion, it's only because our self-esteem is already vulnerable in that area. The gaps in our self-esteem are like chinks in our armour – when someone finds that weak spot, it hurts.

If someone is mean it says everything about them. If we get hurt it says everything about us and how we feel about ourselves. Nobody's opinion need actually hurt you. Nobody need dent your self-esteem. No one should be able to knock your confidence. Of course, that's rarely the case, and when on the receiving end of harsh words or negative opinions we can experience great pain and anguish.

Don't Use Anger To Compensate For Low Self-Esteem

If we respond with anger, that's our self-protection kicking in to compensate for the lack of strength in our self-esteem armour. If self-esteem is our armour, anger is our sword. When our self-esteem is rock solid, not only are we unhurt by comments but we also feel no need to protect ourselves or lash out. The negativity towards us flows off like water off a duck's back.

Not All Criticism Is Equal

The closer the person is to us, the greater capacity their criticism has to hurt us. If we travel back in time through our evolutionary past we find that negative judgement and criticism was meant to be painful. The tribe's acceptance of us meant we were safe. Any negative judgement was intended to pull us into line. If it didn't, we ran the risk of alienation. Back then alienation could easily have meant death. We relied upon the people closest to us to protect us. Therefore, in modern life, if those closest to us don't accept us or approve of us it's far more painful than if a relative stranger doesn't.

Also, the greater the authority of the person judging us, the more it can affect us. The more senior the person in the tribe was, the riskier it would have been to be viewed negatively by them. Their influence meant their opinion counted more than another member of the tribe. They also had disproportionate control of the tribe's resources.

This is why we are driven to please the people closest to us and those who have authority or influence over us. Evolutionarily speaking, it was a perfect strategy for safety. In today's world, it can imprison people in their fear of not being good enough.

Find Your Tribe

Whilst we still have the same responses today, things are very different. We might still rely on each other emotionally but our survival as adults is mostly independent. Tribes in our past were small units and a few members not accepting us or our behaviour was significant. Today, there are many more of us out there willing to accept you for who you really are. The more you are surrounded by people who love, respect and accept you, the less the odd few will matter to you. Also, these positive individuals will breathe life into your self-esteem, making you more resilient to negative people.

Whilst I wouldn't advocate cutting off family and those closest to you, I would advise you to take a good look at those around you and monitor the effect they have on your self-esteem and emotional well-being. You might do well to move away from those who are not particularly important in your life but who are a constant negative force. Those people who are negative but important to you might have to stay close but you don't want to accept the constant negative impact they have on you. Consider bringing about the tough conversations to explain the effect they are having on you and your relationship with them. Work with them to change the dynamic you have between you. They may well not appreciate the conversation and feel attacked themselves, so try to have these talks from a loving, compassionate and non-defensive place. Remember, you're trying to improve the relationship you have with them because you love them.

These conversations can be tough but they are easier when your self-esteem and confidence are strong, so choose your timing. If now isn't the time to bring this up because you feel you can't have this type of conversation with those individuals, consider distancing yourself a little. Once your self-esteem is strong and you have others around you who support what you're doing and who you are being, it will be easier to handle the shorter periods in the firing line of criticism and judgement.

It Only Hurts If You Have A Sore Spot

When our self-esteem is low, anyone and everything has the capacity to slip through our armour and strike deep into our hearts. When our overall self-esteem is higher most of the nonsense just bounces off. However, we all have our vulnerabilities. If someone does hit one of these 'sore spots', instead of feeling bad about yourself or angry at them, try thanking them inwardly for showing you an opportunity to grow. They have shown you something you may not have seen for yourself. As hard as it might be to accept it at the time, that's a gift. It's an opportunity to work on yourself and improve.

Do Your Homework

I know today's content is challenging. If now is the time to act on its lessons, do so. If it isn't, that's okay as well. Go through the Reboot at your own pace. Maybe this part is something to reconsider in the future - nothing I share is meant to be taken as prescriptive. Be mindful of the daily lessons but do as much or as little as you feel is appropriate for you. The real impact over these 28 days comes from the continual application of the daily exercises. So make sure you do yours today and see it through to the very end. Find at least three daily highlights and complete the *I Like Myself...* exercise. Remember your Reminders and don't forget to seek out opportunities to act in alignment with the best of your best traits.

See you tomorrow for our end-of-week check-in.

DAY 21 – Checking In

Just One Week Until Reboot

You know the routine by now – it's time to check in and assess your progress. But before you do, take a moment to acknowledge how awesome you are to get this far. Some people won't make it into the final week, so you should feel proud of yourself. Take a moment to feel good about having stuck to this process. It hasn't always been easy but you've made it.

I know nothing will stop you now!

Checking In

Open your workbook and remind yourself of the Scale you set and your Starting Point on page 229. Also, recap where you were this time last week and complete the Check In for Week 3 on page 231. Draw a line on the scale that you feel represents how you are currently doing. Stay as objective as possible and, as usual, you can use half increments if you feel that better represents where you are at present. Remember, stay consistent with the scale so that you'll be able to accurately measure your progress over the 28 days.

In the space provided, make a list of all the Notable Improvements you've made this past week.

Compare with where you were before. If you've made progress and are feeling better about yourself and maybe more confident, good for you. It's possible you were doing great last check in but feel you've had a bit of a dip this week. This is perfectly normal and nothing to be concerned about. If you've stuck to the whole process and you're still not feeling the full benefit, take comfort in knowing that some people make all the progress in these last seven days.

Don't forget, the support materials will help you at any point you find yourself struggling. The meditations can also have a powerful impact when used over time. If you've fallen off the wagon with any of this, go to: www.BiggerBrighterBolder.co.uk/Reboot/Resources

Regardless of whether you're rocking it, having a dip or generally struggling, please do continue and complete the entire 28 days.

Don't Slack Now

You've done amazing work to get this far but we're not done yet. Continue to follow the process to the letter. Continue with the *I Like Myself...* exercise, the Reminders, and deliberately finding opportunities to align yourself with those highlighted themes in your Deliberate Action List.

Now you have another week of data it might be worth going through your recent *I Like Myself...* highlights, looking for patterns to make sure you're still taking action on the right themes. You might feel you need to add another or swap one out. This is fine as you go into your final week.

During the week ahead, I won't keep reminding you to continue to complete the *I Like myself...* exercise or to add to your Reminders. If you've got this far, you already know how important they are. The Reminders will serve you beyond the

Reboot. They will act as an abbreviation of your entire 28-day experience and act as a great recap in the future.

One More Week

There are just seven days until we complete our journey together. Once again, well done for getting this far – I take my hat off to you.

Keep showing up!

I'll see you tomorrow.

DAY 22 – Staying Motivated

You've come this far so I have every faith that you will complete this programme. But the Reboot is not just for these 28 days. You'll want to continue with this journey.

Whether it's continuing to work on your self-esteem or undertaking anything else that requires consistent significant effort, you need to be able to manage your motivation levels.

Lower levels of self-esteem will lower motivation. If we don't deserve something our subconscious will not let us fully commit to its attainment. Equally, if we doubt our abilities or the outcome, motivation will be unconsciously withheld. One of the most frequent questions I get is about how to stay motivated.

If I Could Bottle It

Being motivated simply means wanting to do something and having the right emotional chemistry flowing to move you forward to achieve it. On a good day we awake inspired and fired up. On another, it takes all we've got to get out of bed in the morning. It feels like motivation is something that comes and goes – as if it happens *to* us. Life is easier when we're motivated. We inherently know this and are painfully aware when it's lacking. If I could bottle motivation, I'd sell it and make a fortune.

Motivation Is Within You

The motivation you've lost or which seems to be missing is inside you. It's always been there. Motivation happens *within* us. It's an emotional response based on our subconscious processing the available data stored as previous experiences and learning, plus our perceptions in the moment. It might feel random but it's not, and there are things we can do to keep motivation flowing.

The Purpose Of Motivation

Motivation, like all emotions, has evolved to manipulate our actions. When something is unconsciously perceived as good for us, it triggers the release of motivation to manipulate us to go get it. However, even if the subconscious calculates something is good for us, if there is a perceived threat to its attainment, motivation won't be triggered. We may desire something but consider it potentially harmful. The two opposing forces may cancel each other out. In our evolutionary past, this might have been a source of food being guarded by a wild bear. Today, it might be desiring to be financially successful but holding onto an unconscious concept that money corrupts. Another threat might be the perceived effort needed to attain something. You might want it, but you'll have no motivation if the effort versus reward isn't perceived as worthwhile.

Be Reward Focused

Throughout this programme I've been encouraging you to acknowledge any positive changes you've witnessed, no matter how small. It's these little rewards that show the subconscious that what you're putting energy into is paying off. If you disregard these rewards as inconsequential whilst also perceiving the process as challenging, the subconscious may weigh up the effort as not worth it and pull the plug on motivation. This is why it's so important to feel great about all the little rewards along the journey. If we're waiting for the big payoff before acknowledging the rewards for our effort, our subconscious is unlikely to keep us motivated long enough to achieve it.

The Short-Term Focus Of The Subconscious

A major factor in anyone's success, in any area of life, is their ability to apply themselves to a high degree for a sustained amount of time. However, if you struggle to commit yourself to the success you want in life, it's not your fault.

Once again, if we take a trip back through our evolutionary past we find all of our problems were short-term ones. Getting enough food for the day and keeping ourselves safe from the many things that would harm us was a full-time job. No point in thinking about tomorrow if we didn't make it through today. As we evolved into early farmers, we started to invest ourselves for rewards we would reap in the future. This was a huge leap forward from our hunter-gatherer past but only occurred some ten to twenty-thousand years ago. For the vast majority of our past we were opportunistic and short-term focused, and that bias remains to this day. Therefore we need a constant stream of perceived short-term rewards in order to play the longer game required to create a more fulfilling life.

The Promise Of Big Rewards

On Day 19 I shared the importance of being goal focused and having dreams in life. Whilst the promise of big rewards is often what gives us the initial kick of motivation to get us started, it isn't long until the subconscious starts to realise that those rewards are a long way off and require a lot of effort. It's the combination of being connected to the promise of big, long-term rewards, coupled with the constant acknowledgement of smaller, short-term gains, that keeps us motivated.

The Last Person In The River

An analogy I often share to explain the relationship between short-term reward, motivation and winning the long game is what I call, 'The last person in the river'.

It's 1850 and we're in California, USA. The gold rush is in full swing and we hear that, "There is gold in that there river." Despite this, many don't make the trip as they don't believe it exists, so what's the point? However, you, me and a gang of others go down to the river seeking our fortunes.

After a few hard days, we're cold wet and tired, and morale starts to wane. As sieve after sieve returns nothing but mud, dirt and stone, some of our once-motivated gang pack up and go home. They no longer believe there is gold in the river, so what's the point? However, you, me and some others stay on, working tirelessly in the pursuit of our destiny. We still believe there is gold to be found.

More days pass and we're getting hungry and exhausted. All the hard work with no reward is starting to become wearing, even for the most optimistic of us. There are increasing murmurs of doubt amongst those left. More go home as they lose their faith in finding any gold. As they put it, "What would be the point in staying?" Just a handful of us remain.

Then you see it. Almost invisible to the eye, you see a tiny fleck of gold. You sift more of the river bed and see more. You question whether you're just starting to find it or if it's been there the entire time, being overlooked as you searched for larger nuggets of gold. You look over people's shoulders and notice that every sieve clearly contains these tiny flecks. They amount to nothing much but what you now know for sure is that there is gold in this river. As if by magic, you no longer feel as weary as you did. You barely notice your hunger and this discovery gives you a new lease of life. But no one else is acknowledging this gold. You can't believe they're not seeing it.

More time passes.

We lose the remainder of our gang to promises of warm beds and hot food back in town. They give up. After weeks, they believe they've found nothing. What would be the point of them staying on? In the end, just you and I remain. You seem to have a second wind as I feel increasingly tired, despondent and disillusioned. I'm close to giving up, too. You decide to do me a favour and point out the tiny, shiny flecks in our pans. At first I can't see anything but then I spot them - barely visible to the naked eye. I take this in and then say, "Are you fricking kidding me?! Is that it?! I've been alongside you in the river for weeks now. I'm hungry, tired, wet and thoroughly fed up. I can't believe I went through all that. For what? For a worthless tiny speck?"

I throw my pan in the river and go back to town. I encourage you to do the same, saying, "What's the point?"

Bemused, you watch me ride back to town. You're confused because whilst the flecks of gold don't amount to much, they clearly show you there is gold in this river. Spurred on by the morsels of reward and the ongoing promise of your fortune, you stay.

And then you get what you knew was possible – a perfect little nugget of gold. It's not huge but this is worth something and clearly there is more gold to be had. This proves to be true as you start to pick up more and more of the valuable nuggets. And they get increasingly bigger.

You start loading the gold into the saddlebags of your horse. Then you fill your pockets. Once you've stashed as much as you and your horse can possibly carry, you head back to town – exhausted, but fully rewarded for your efforts. As you arrive, we all come out to greet you. And at the sight of your huge windfall, together we proclaim, "You lucky bastard!"

The moral of this story is that the last person standing in the river gets all the gold, and when you've worked your arse off and done all the things others weren't prepared to do, people will often ignore your efforts, persistence and tenacity and write it off as merely a matter of luck. The notion it was luck, and not a failing of theirs, helps them sleep at night.

See The Gold

Continue taking time to positively reflect on all the flecks of gold in your life. The *I Like Myself...* exercise helps you with this. But that is just the beginning. There is gold everywhere. It's always been there but maybe you've just been seeing the crap and sludge. Maybe you've been searching for the big nuggets of gold and missed all the flecks that are always there. Maybe you're tired and starting to wonder whether there's any point. Know there is gold in the river of your life. If you acknowledge it, you'll stay motivated long enough to find all that is available to you – both the tiny flecks and the huge nuggets.

What's The Point?

The enemy of maintained motivation is any version of, "What's the point?" You might hear the words in your head or just feel it, but when you perceive there is no point your subconscious pulls the plug on motivation. From there it is only a matter of time until you give up.

Never Give Up!

It's all to play for – you might just need to stand in the river a little longer.

See you tomorrow.

DAY 23 – Resilience

Just 5 Days Until Reboot

As you head towards the end of this programme we need to make sure you're able to maintain all the gains made to your self-esteem. I've referred to your self-esteem as a suit of armour. During this process of strengthening it, I've given you permission to protect yourself. You will want to continue to do that, as required, beyond the Reboot. However, eventually you won't need to protect yourself at all. Any hits that come your way will bounce off.

Resilience

Resilience is the capacity to recover quickly from setbacks and difficulties – in other words, it's your toughness.

Even with the best will in the world, we all have to face challenges and difficulties in life. Our resilience is our ability to be unaffected by these. This doesn't mean that resilient people don't have their wobbles. We all do. It just means they possess the ability to bounce back.

We need to be able to bounce back from our setbacks, too. We need to be able to come back, regroup and fight again after our losses. We need to keep moving forward in the face of whatever obstacles get in our way. It's not the ease of the journey but our strength and courage to continue that determines our success.

Tennis Anyone?

The knack to keeping yourself on top of external challenges that might knock you off your game is to centre yourself in a space of perceived safety. This is the mental and emotional space where you are strong, calm and at ease with yourself.

I liken this space to the T spot on a tennis court. Whilst a good tennis player can play from anywhere on the court and some have their own preferences, you'll often see them gravitate back to the T. If their opponent sends them to the back of the court with a deep shot, you can bet the next shot will be close to the net. If the player runs to the net in expectation of that shot, you can bet their opponent will send the ball back to the baseline. By resetting back to the T they can cover the entire court. Chasing the ball around the court is a sure-fire way of exhausting yourself, playing into your opponent's game and almost certainly losing.

Your T is where you can best cover the metaphorical court of your life. Things will inevitably arise to pull or push you out of that space. Your job is to reset as quickly as possible. If you don't, you'll end up off your own game and running around in reaction to the world around you.

Identifying Your Safe Space

When you become familiar with your personal T you'll know when you're on it and when you're being pushed or pulled away from it.

Exercise

The following exercise will help you find your T. This exercise should be done when you feel strong and safe, which is why I've left this topic until the last week of the Reboot. Making a note of your answers in the Reminders section of your workbook, complete the following statements. You don't need to limit yourself to just one response.

- What I like most about myself is...
- If someone doesn't like me, it doesn't matter because...
- Making mistakes is okay because...
- Not being perfect is okay because...
- The most important things in my life are...
- The dream I'm committed to creating is...
- The person I am becoming is...
- I trust myself because...

Living life from this place makes you strong and feel safe. If anything in life moves you away from it you know where you need to reset back to. The more often you reset yourself to your space of certainty, strength and confidence, the easier it will be to do.

The More You Take, The Tougher You Get

Tough situations and challenges can break us down and, going back to our boxer analogy from Day 3, knock us out. However, there's truth in the saying, "What doesn't kill us makes us stronger." This programme is about protecting yourself while you Reboot your self-esteem. But once you are strong enough to step back in the ring, those knocks are the very thing that will strengthen you further.

The more we're able to overcome what life throws at us, the tougher we become. Like training at the gym, the harder the session is the stronger we get. So be grateful for the challenges of the past for making you who you are today. Moving forward, don't wish for challenges and difficulties in life, but when they show up, embrace the opportunity to grow and strengthen more. Your future tough-as-nails self will be grateful for those times of resilience building.

Getting Back In The Ring

If you're feeling up to it, now might be the time to consider putting yourself back in the firing line of some of the challenging spaces and people we identified back on Day 3. However, tread carefully and slowly and don't feel bad if you feel the need to protect yourself for a little longer. If you're unsure whether you're ready or not, give yourself some more time. This is not a race and you do not want to undo anything you've worked so hard to create over the past few weeks. There's always tomorrow.

DAY 24 – Standing Your Ground And Owning Your Space

Just 4 Days Until Reboot

Today's challenge is to stand your ground. This can be really tough for people with low levels of self-esteem. However, you're coming towards the end of the Reboot and feeling better about yourself. I'm inviting you, if you feel up to it, to start exerting yourself more fully in the world around you.

Be Strong But Don't Be A Dick

This is not about being belligerent or rude – it's not about being a dick. It's about being who it's important for you to be for yourself. It's about doing and creating what's important for you. It's about saying "No" when you mean no. I've been encouraging this slowly throughout the Reboot.

Speaking Your Mind

If you find yourself in company where you don't agree with what's being said, you don't have to jump up and shout, "I think you're wrong." You might simply choose not to engage in that conversation. But if there's a part of you which feels as if you should speak up and it would damage your self-esteem not to, you might want to express yourself. You needn't feel the urge to share every thought you have, just what's important to you.

This is about daring to speak up when before you wouldn't, and would have felt bad for not doing so. When you honour yourself in this way you'll feel better, and become stronger and more confident. It will boost your self-esteem. If you're not feeling up to this challenge right now, that's fine. Put this lesson to one side and come back to it later when you feel a little stronger.

Dancing Around Like A Bloody Ballerina

When out and about, own the physical space you occupy. Stand tall and strong. As a people pleaser and someone who still goes through cycles of lower self-esteem, I can fall foul of this one. Not so long ago I was in Dubai, by the fountains near the Burj Khalifa where the crowds are often large. On this occasion there was a steady stream of people walking straight at me. I didn't want to knock into anyone so was dodging out of everyone's way. I'm a big strong guy but I was dancing around like a bloody ballerina, constantly apologising. Then I remembered this lesson in the Reboot. I remembered my own words. Without being a dick or throwing my weight around, I started walking purposefully, owning my space.

When you bump shoulders it's a two-way thing. You're both bumping shoulders. It's not just your responsibility to avoid this. In this instance, I simply started walking in my own straight line. Every now and then I would move aside because it was the right thing to do. But generally, I stood my ground and a funny thing happened – *they* started dancing around *me* like ballerinas! Again, this isn't about being a dick, and of course I politely move out of people's way. But in this case, for my own self-worth, it was right for me to step into my space of strength and confidence.

Have Fun With It

I know it might sound like an unimportant thing, but actually, if you think about the psychology behind dancing around everyone else and always apologising, that doesn't sound like someone who's exerting themselves or owning their space in the world. In that moment it was important for me to remind myself, "I deserve my space – I own this space."

If you're a person who ends up dancing like a ballerina like I did, try holding your ground. Hold your space. Don't be a knob about it but understand that this is your space as well. Always giving way or apologising can be a sign of low self-esteem. Hold your ground, metaphorically and perhaps physically as well. Treat it like an experiment and see how changing your approach alters how others react to you and how you feel as a result. Have fun with it. This is a playful and literal way of demonstrating something much more significant – owning your place in this world.

As always with these challenges, if you're not quite up for it yet, come back to it later.

DAY 25 – Action Beats Reaction

Just 3 Days Until Reboot

You're almost at the end so I'm deliberately turning up the heat. Make sure you see the daily exercises through to the very last day. Continue with the *I Like Myself...* exercise and keep proactively looking for those opportunities to align your actions with your Deliberate Action List. If you haven't done one for a while, maybe dig out your favourite of the meditations/visualisations.

Run Your Own Race

All the way along this Reboot journey I've been suggesting you live life on your terms and I've shared this concept in many ways. Compromising on who you're being or what you're achieving is a sure-fire way to lessen self-esteem and live a life of regret. Of course, there are others you share your life with and they must be taken into consideration, but overall you must create a life of your choosing. The aim is to have others around you benefit from that and support you in achieving it.

Athletes must run their own race. Being pulled into a competitor's tactics only plays into the other person's agenda, thereby weakening their own. A common tactic in longer distance running is to try and dictate how the race is run. For example, if an athlete is a fast-paced, consistent runner, they will prefer to push the pace throughout the race so as to negate a sprint-finisher's desire to leave the push to the end.

A heavy-hitting, larger boxer might prefer to stand toe-to-toe and slug it out, whereas a faster, lighter boxer will have a desire to hit and move. If either forgets their own strategy and gets pulled into the other's fight, it only serves their opponent.

Action Beats Reaction

In my distant past I taught self-defence and kickboxing.
Whilst both require very different strategies, they shared one
significant similarity – set the agenda! One of the mantras I'd
repeat ad nauseam was, "Action beats reaction!" Whether in
the ring or on the street, they were to set the agenda and get
their opponent on their plan and not the other way around. As
a general rule in self-defence, if it ever came to them having
to physically defend themselves, they shouldn't wait to be hit
first. Far better to have an aggressor react to them than play
catch-up with their assailant. This was just a tiny segment of
a complete self-defence strategy so please don't take this as
instruction for what to do yourself.

Life Is Not A Fight

But of course, you're not in a race, competition or fight with
anyone. These merely serve as analogies about why it's
important to be on your own path. If you're not on your agenda
you're probably on someone else's. If one person is committed
to their vision, direction and goals and another is aimless, the

latter will almost certainly end up serving the former's agenda. To be blunt, you're either a pilot or a passenger in your life.

The starting point of this programme was to Reboot your levels of self-esteem. The end point is to set you up for living and creating a fulfilling life, lived on your terms.

DAY 26 – Don't Be Afraid Of Your Secrets

Just 2 Days Until Reboot

Your Secrets Are Holding You Back

Any secrets you have that you fear people finding out about have a hold over you. They hold you back and they lower your levels of self-esteem. I want you to start thinking about letting some of these secrets out into the world. This is not for the faint-hearted and I don't recommend you reveal everything straight away.

When my children were born, my relationship with their mother was not a good one. When my babies were still small, just months old, I made the very tough decision to leave that relationship. For years I felt terrible about myself. I shared the story of my guilt on Day 13. I can look back on this now and say that it was the right decision for everybody concerned. At the time I couldn't see it. I felt guilty. I felt like a terrible human being and, worst of all, I felt like a failure as a dad.

Around the same time, the business I ran also failed. I had these two huge and shameful secrets. As I saw things at the time, I was a terrible father, a terrible human being and a complete and utter fucking failure in every area of my life. Holding onto these feelings about myself gave others permission to see me that way too.

Own Your Secrets Or They'll Own You

I came to realise that by holding onto my secrets and being so ashamed of them, they had a hold over me. I always feared that someone was going to find out and judge me harshly – as harshly as I was judging myself. It was causing me massive emotional discomfort and harming my ability to connect with others.

So I began sharing them. Initially it was only where I felt safest. Then I'd share in wider circles. Eventually, I got to the point where I would walk into a group of new people and introduce myself by saying, "Hi, I'm George," and within a few sentences add, "I've left my kids' mother and my business just failed." I literally threw it out there. I'll be honest with you, I was probably guilty of oversharing but it stopped these secrets from being my 'dark' secrets. By sharing them so candidly people responded in the same manner. I owned my secrets and they stopped owning me.

People Take Their Lead From You

When you feel something is a big dark secret to be ashamed of, other people will treat it the same way. But if you share it like it's nothing, others will react accordingly.

An extreme example of this comes from a previous client of mine. He had some incredibly dark secrets which he was so ashamed of that he couldn't consider sharing them with anyone. In fact, I didn't know the full extent of his secrets until months into our coaching. I helped him process his past and make peace with it. Eventually, they became part of his incredible transformation story which he now shares freely with anyone who will listen. He realised that whilst his past was not what he would choose, it was what made him who he is today and what gave him an incredible opportunity to be a positive force in this world. The shame he once felt is actually part of an incredibly inspiring story. When he shares his 'secrets' in that way, his audience reacts in kind. The negative judgement he feared actually ended up being admiration and respect.

Another client was a woman who's past held many secrets. Even her husband of twenty years had no idea about these. Through a process similar to the previous example, she not only made her peace with her own demons but went on to write a book about them and has spoken about this on stage in front of hundreds of people.

Both of these individuals are now free from their secrets. But more than that, they are empowered, inspirational figures with great confidence and self-esteem.

Dare To Let Go Of Your Secrets

I want you to start looking at your own secrets – the things you're ashamed of that you hide from the world and that make you hide from the world. Holding onto them is allowing them to have a hold over you. I'm not suggesting you should go out into the world and share everything with everyone right now. But consider what life might look like if you followed the examples set out above.

Letting go of my secrets freed me in many ways. At the time of writing this I have been coaching and mentoring businesses for over a decade and have personally worked with over 500 business owners. Can you imagine the hold my business failure from twenty years ago would have over me if I'd kept it as my dark secret? I don't believe I would have got this far, cowering in the shadows, waiting to be found out as the fraud and failure my fears at the time led me to believe I was.

Process First, Share Second

First you must make peace with your secrets. Like those in the examples above, you must own your story. Realise that whilst things from your past might not be what you would now choose, they are nothing to be ashamed of. They are part of the story of who you are today. When you let go of the shame and make peace with your secrets, you can begin to share them.

If They Don't Like It, Stuff Them

Once you're in a good place with your once dark secrets, anyone who feeds back to you negatively about your story can get stuffed. It says everything about them and nothing about you. But you should not share your story until you feel this way yourself. Until then, continue processing your secrets privately.

Up For The Challenge?

It's not necessary to go out there and share before you're ready. I had worked with the guy above for a number of months before he was anywhere near ready to share any details of his past. But understand that these secrets of yours have a hold over you. They are holding you back.

Exercise

- What secrets are you holding onto that have a hold over you?
- What are you most scared of if people find out?
- What are the positives you can take from these secrets that make you who you are today?

Maybe it's time to ask which is more important - to protect yourself from people who don't know or understand you, or to authentically be yourself?

Perhaps it's time to start daring to let some of your secrets out. People may or may not judge you, but hey, stuff them. That's their business, right? Your business is to create the life that you want. If you feel ready now, or when you feel ready in the future, start letting some of those secrets out. Don't be afraid of them. The fear they hold over you is the only thing that fuels them.

DAY 27 – The Antidote To Fear

Just 1 Day Until Reboot

Fear Creates More Harm Than Good

Fear is our response to physical threat. In our evolutionary past it served us well. Even until recent times, life was hard and fear still served us. But life today is not that unsafe. The threats we face are rarely life-threatening yet fear is still the dominant emotion in our lives. Out in the wild, where every day is a battle for survival and safety, fear protects. In our evolutionary past, the fear of not having enough food or shelter, and even the fear of not being good enough, protected us. But now it harms far more than it serves us.

Fear Shuts You Down

Our fear response is often described as our fight or flight response. In fact, it would be more accurately described as our fight, flight or freeze response. However, neither accurately represents how things typically pan out. The most accurate real-world description would be flight if at all possible, freeze if not, and as an absolute last resort when we're cornered (metaphorically or literally), fight.

Even those wild animals that we perceive as being most aggressive are more likely to flee or back down from a physically threatening situation. Lions, gorillas and polar bears would all rather walk away from a fight than risk getting injured or killed. Even these beasts, with their potential for extreme violence, prefer to posture and perform rather than engage in an actual and risky fight. We are no different.

We are much more likely to retreat from our threats rather than engage with them. It's also more likely that our threats are perceived threats rather than actual ones. And in our modern world those threats are rarely physical. However, the subconscious cannot differentiate between a non-physical and physical threat and responds to both in the same way.

Most of our problems today require creative solutions, not physical ones. But our hard-wired physical threat responses actually shut down our creativity. In fact, the more intense our fear, the less we are able to access those aspects of ourselves that are most capable of solving our modern-day problems.

Fear switches on our anger and attack response and switches off compassion, sympathy, empathy, cognitive thinking, communication, creativity and fine judgement. It also limits our ability to interpret others' intentions and makes us much more likely to respond with distrust and hostility.

The greater the fear, the more we shut down.

Control

Under the influence of fear, we tend to run, bury our head in the sand or, if cornered, attack. However, we also have a tendency to try to control everything. This desire for control is born out of our underlying fear. Again, if we go back through the ages this makes sense. Taking control of a situation that could cause us harm protected us. Today we have lost none of that desire to gain control of the world around us and over those with whom we occupy it. Our craving for control is fuelled by, and symptomatic of, our fear. We therefore won't eradicate our fear through control.

The Antidote To Fear

The antidote to much of our fear is trust. When we can't have certainty, which is often the case, trust is the crutch we can lean upon to support us into the unknown. What is unknown to us is perceived as unsafe and that which is known, safe. Therefore, our unconscious insatiable appetite for safety keeps us locked into the known and resists change. Our subconscious' preoccupation with safety holds us back from all that could be. Trust allows us to venture into possibility.

The Greatest Gift You Can Give Yourself

Our craving for safety trumps any desire we have for happiness and success. Thus, what *is* is often calculated as far safer than what *could be* – even when the former is terrible and the latter terrific. Therefore, the greatest gift we can give ourselves is the perception and sense of safety and security. Trust is the vehicle for this. If we don't learn to trust in ourselves and that which is around us, our subconscious will satisfy its craving for safety by holding us back and stopping us from progressing.

The Triangle Of Trust

In order to feel safe in this world, there are three areas of life you need to trust in.

Firstly, you need to trust in yourself. You need to have faith that you are good enough. You need to trust yourself to get through whatever you face in life. You need to trust that you're doing the best you can and that if ever that's not enough, you are still okay.

Secondly, trust in humanity.

This can be hard for many as this isn't just about trusting those nearest and dearest. This is about trusting in the human collective. Trusting that all people, like you, are trying their best. And, just like you, occasionally their best won't be good enough. Not everyone will act and behave in ways that you would like them to. Not everyone does the right thing. But we must trust in our collective humanity. We are often divided over issues but when we break through these we all share common desires and values. Don't let the few things we disagree upon get in the way of the vast amount of commonality we share.

Lastly, we must trust in something bigger than ourselves. If you are religious, this might be your deity. If spiritual, it could be your trust in the universe. If you're an atheist, it could be your connection to the natural order of things or the science of nature.

The end result is feeling supported and taken care of by your own self, huminty and something beyond that. I typically write these three at the points of an equilateral triangle. I refer to this as the Triangle of Trust.

Your Triangle of Trust cannot rely on just one or two sides. A strong trust in yourself, while hugely beneficial, will not be able to compensate for a total lack of trust in humanity. Likewise, trusting in others will not fully compensate for your lack of self-trust. All three sides of an equilateral triangle are of equal length. This is what gives it its incredible strength and stability. Take a look at how you might be able to strengthen the weaker sides of your triangle.

Look For Evidence

There is proof all around you that you can trust in these three things. If you seek the reassurance that you can trust in life, you will find it. Equally, if you only tune into the evidence that says you can't trust, that's the reality you will perceive. I assure you, there is far more evidence that you can trust in yourself, others and something bigger than that you can't. Acknowledge this as often as you can. Forgive yourself, others or events in life when that trust is broken. You are always trying the best you can, as is everyone else, even when you or they fail to deliver – sometimes spectacularly.

Exercise

Please answer the following:

- Why can you trust yourself?
- Where is your evidence for that?
- Why, on the whole, can you trust other people?
- Where is the evidence for that?
- What can you trust in that's bigger than you?
- Why can you trust that?
- Where is the evidence for that?

Make a note of what you need to remember in your list of Reminders.

Trust is Your Safety Net

When you can't be certain of an outcome, trust it will be okay. And more than that, trust that even when it isn't okay, you are still safe. Ultimately, if you trust that you are safe, even when everything around you could make you think otherwise, you will have the secure base you need to keep your fear at bay and you moving forward.

DAY 28 – Congratulations!

Reboot Completed!

Whoop! Whoop! Whoop!

Hello, and for the very last time, welcome to The 28-Day Self-Esteem Reboot. Your Reboot is complete! Just take a moment to feel fantastic about that. Imagine the party poppers, streamers, balloons and champagne corks flying – you deserve a well-earned celebration in honour of your absolute awesomeness.

Pat yourself on the back and acknowledge the journey we've been on over the past 28 days. There have been highs and I'm sure some lows, but you consistently turned up day after day. Do not ignore how great an achievement it is that you have stuck with this programme to the very end. Whilst I have created and designed the Reboot to get everyone across the finish line, I don't kid myself that everyone will. You are why I created this. You are what makes this so worthwhile for me.

We've come a long way, you and I. Maybe at the beginning you weren't too sure whether you could trust me or this process. Maybe you were sceptical but hopeful about the ability of the Reboot to deliver.

I'm hoping that over this month you've come to realise that I only want the very best for you and your life. I feel we have a special bond here, even though we might not have met in person. I truly respect you for completing this programme.

So congratulations on seeing it through and thank you for allowing this programme to deliver its purpose. A huge round of applause for getting here! You are bloody awesome!

Checking In

You know what to do. Open your workbook and remind yourself of the Scale you set and your Starting Point on page 229. And once again, recap where you were this time last week. Then complete the Check In for Week 4 on page 231. Draw a line on the scale that you feel represents where you have got to on this Reboot. Stay as objective as possible and, as always, use half increments if you feel that better represents where you are at present. As long as you've used the same scale you will have accurately measured your progress over the last 28 days.

In the space provided, make a list of all the Notable Improvements you've made this past week.

Reflect

Now reflect on the past 28 days. Think about all those *I Like Myself...* statements and highlights over the past 4 weeks. If you've kept up with the three-a-day minimum, that's at least 84 in total! That is a huge number of successes to feel proud of. If you add to that the last two weeks of proactively aligning with your Deliberate Action List, and if you've been taking action on the challenges that I've set you, it's an incredible achievement.

Go back and remember all those specks of gold – all those little improvements – those little successes that are so easy to overlook and downplay. They add up. Of course, acknowledge the bigger nuggets of gold as well.

Before And After

Open your workbook and turn to Before on pages 232. Take a moment and cast your eye over where you were just 28 days ago when you first set out. Reconnect with where you were at the beginning of your journey and take stock of how far you've come. Acknowledge where you feel better about yourself, where you're presenting yourself to the world in better ways and where you're feeling more confident.

Now take a moment to acknowledge just how far you've come. Maybe you've really surprised yourself on this journey. Hopefully, it's been positive from start to finish, even if a little challenging at times. Take time to reflect on who you were before, how you thought and felt, and who you are today.

You may find you've made small incremental changes in some areas but huge leaps forward in others. All these changes, great and small, will have contributed to your greater levels of self-esteem and confidence. Perhaps you're not quite seeing it yet, but you will. Take a moment to enjoy all these improvements.

Grab a pen and fill out the After section on page 233. Build a picture of where you are right now as a snapshot. You might do a direct comparison, looking at where you were before and comparing to where you are now, or you might look at the whole and rewrite it from your current point of view.

- Where have you improved?
- Where and how have you been positively exerting yourself?
- Where have you held your ground and been a bit more fearless?
- How have your thoughts changed?
- How are you feeling?
- How are you expressing yourself differently in the world around you?
- How is the world starting to interact with you more positively?

Don't Stop Now

Continue with your Reboot. Whilst you've come to the end the programme, there's nothing stopping you from continuing with the exercises. I would absolutely encourage you to continue. Go beyond the Reboot and continue to grow your levels of self-esteem. Continue with the *I Like Myself...* exercise. Continue to update and proactively apply those Deliberate Actions. Keep updating your list of Reminders and continue to look at it daily.

Look back at the lessons that you've received throughout this programme and increasingly exert yourself powerfully and authentically.

- Continue to say no.
- Only say yes when you mean yes.
- Express yourself fully.
- Be braver, be bolder, be more courageous.
- Stop being who you think you should be.
- Start being who you want to be.
- Continue to create yourself by your own design.
- Have more faith and trust in yourself.
- Continue to acknowledge the positive in yourself.

- Forgive yourself when you need to.
- Raise your game but stop trying to be perfect.
- Make yourself a priority.
- Block out negativity.
- Surround yourself with positivity.
- Be kind to yourself.
- Stop judging others.
- Regularly demonstrate your love for yourself.

Continue to push yourself to the next level of self-esteem. Remember, you cannot have too much self-esteem and the attributes often negatively associated with having high levels, such as arrogance and conceit, are actually expressions of low self-esteem. With great self-esteem you only express yourself in positive ways. You have a massive positive impact on the world around you. You have nothing to prove. You stand firm and strong in who you are, what you believe in and what you're creating.

Beyond Reboot

So often in life, we take these challenges and, at the end of them, move on and forget the lessons we fought hard to learn. You were on this Reboot because you identified as wanting greater levels of self-esteem. That takes a lot of bravery in the first place.

If you continue with the momentum you've built over the last 28 days you will continue to grow and your life will improve with it. Remember, every aspect of your life will improve with greater levels of self-esteem.

Exercise

Open your workbook to page 234, Beyond Reboot. Write down all the things you want to create from here on. Maybe it's taking your confidence and self-esteem to the next level – what does that look like? What have you been putting off that you now feel like progressing? What goals do you want to achieve? What changes do you want to make? What do you want the rest of your life to look like? Write as much as you need to about what you want from your future.

CONGRATULATIONS!

By completing the entire 28 days, you have unlocked the Beyond Reboot bonus content. I have recorded some extra lessons and another visualisation. You can find the link in the Bonus Material section at:
www.BiggerBrighterBolder.co.uk/Reboot/Resources.

Use the code NEXTLEVEL to gain access.

Ding-Ding – Round Two?

Why not go again? You could continue with just the daily exercises or you can turn back to page one and start afresh. From a position of greater self-esteem you will hear the lessons from a new, more empowered perspective. You'll be able to push yourself a little harder than you did the first time around and it will work every subsequent time you engage with it. You can purchase another workbook at:
www.BiggerBrighterBolder.co.uk/Reboot/Resources.

Continuing Our Journey

We've come a long way and we can still continue our journey together. I'd like to introduce you to other ways I can support your ongoing drive to improve yourself and create a wonderful life.

The Wheel Of Life

My Wheel Of Life tool is proven to improve overall happiness and fulfilment and is an excellent follow up to the Reboot. It guides you through 12 months of self-coaching for improving all areas of life. It's simple, but extremely effective. Once it has been initially set up, it only takes a small amount of time on a weekly and monthly basis, and will assist you in improving your health, wellbeing, work, money, family, friends and intimate relationships. The real beauty of the process is that while it guides you to look at these areas, you and you alone determine what you want. I talk throughout the Reboot of creating yourself by design and building the life you want, with the Wheel Of Life, you get to do exactly that. If you want to take your new and improved self-esteem and apply it in your life, you can find out more at:
www.BiggerBrighterBolder.co.uk/wheel-of-life

Success Groups

If you run your own business or are thinking of launching a business, remember my day job is supporting ambitious small business owners in taking their businesses to the next level. Whether you're in the process of launching your new business, wanting to build your business to 100K annual turnover, or if you already have a turnover of between 100K and 500K, and want to scale, we have groups of ambitious business owners just like you, doing those very things.

My Success Groups are a one-stop shop, offering a complete toolkit to build the business you want and boost your earnings. Our members enjoy all the benefits of courses, books, peer group support and coaching for a fraction of the cost of doing these things individually.

Success Groups has a proven track record since 2012,

building small businesses into more fulfilling, more profitable and more owner-friendly organisations. You can find out more at: www.BiggerBrighterBolder.co.uk, or you can email us directly: Live@BiggerBrighterBolder.co.uk

Get More Out Of Me

If you own a business, I have many resources to help you grow including my Levelling Up podcast, workshops and my small business philosophy book. You can find all these links as well those for my social media channels in the Feeling Inspired section immediately following this.

I'd love to think that this was just the beginning of our relationship, not the end.

Once again, well done and congratulations on seeing it through. This is the beginning of the rest of your life.

- Happiness and Success Start with Self-Esteem.

Pass it on

When you've finished with this book, feel free to pass it on to someone who you feel would benefit from it. However, if you've become attached to this copy and want to hold onto it, please forward the following link to those you recommend this programme to so they can purchase their own copy: www.BiggerBrighterBolder.co.uk/Reboot.

Feeling Inspired?

Take Your Business To The Next Level

SUCCESS
GROUPS ➤

LAUNCH BUILD SCALE

George's day job is coaching, mentoring and leading small business owners to greater levels of success.

If you feel inspired to step up and accept the challenge of creating the business and success you've always desired, George would love to introduce you to his Success Groups. Whether you are in the early phases of launching your business, in the process of building your business to 100K turnover, or you have a successful business achieving over 100K and want to scale, there'll be a perfect group of highly-motivated, like-minded peers waiting to welcome you.

To find out more, email:
Live@BiggerBrighterBolder.co.uk
or go to:
www.BiggerBrighterBolder.co.uk

The Wheel Of Life

An excellent follow up to your Reboot. The Wheel of Life takes you through a year of self-coaching, looking at improving the overall quality of all areas of life. You can find out more at: www.BiggerBrighterBolder.co.uk/wheel-of-life

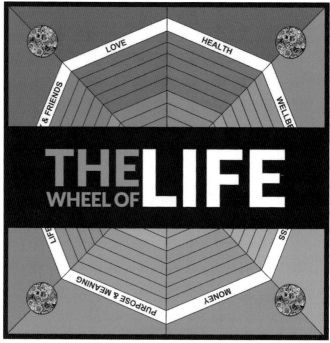

Balancing The Entrepreneur Within

Within each and every one of us there are multiple and often conflicting personality traits. We want to be bold, yet we play it safe. We need to step into the light, yet we hide in the shadows. Our business needs us to take more interest in its finances, yet we find it so boring! Struggles like these are not at all unusual.

This complete workshop in a box helps you to identify your own winning formula by balancing these conflicting traits into a single, harmonised and successful entrepreneurial personality. www.BiggerBrighterBolder.co.uk/balancing

67 Kick-Arse Philosophies For Small Business Owners

Small businesses don't fail, their owners do. 67 Kick-arse Philosophies is a nonsense-free guide to personal performance and business growth.

Find out more at:
www.BiggerBrighterBolder.co.uk/67

Levelling Up with George Swift

Subscribe to George's business podcast. You can find it on iTunes, Spotify, SoundCloud and other podcast directories. You can also find it at:
www.BiggerBrighterBolder.co.uk/levelling-up-podcast

Big Shout Out

Tracey Miller, for co-creating Bigger Brighter Bolder with me – our beautiful, bouncing, business baby.

Rachel Tapping, for her invaluable help in turning my written ramblings into something worth reading. www.racheltapping.com

Chantal Bourgonje, for the typesetting, layout and internal design. www.cfordesign.co.uk

Annie Hall, for the cover design. www.phase-two.co.uk

My daughters, Georgia and Olivia, for reflecting the best that's in me.

My Mum, who was such an amazing supporter of mine, throughout the ups and downs of my crazy life.

Finally, a big thank you to everyone who has been through this programme and therefore helped shape it into what it is today.

THE 28 DAY
SELF-ESTEEM
REBOOT

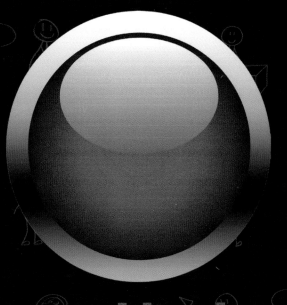

workbook

Index

REMINDERS

REMINDERS

REMINDERS

REMINDERS

REMINDERS

REMINDERS

REMINDERS

REMINDERS

DAY 1

Highlight and why
_____
_____
_____

My part
_____
_____
_____

I like myself because
_____
_____
_____

Highlight and why
_____
_____
_____

My part
_____
_____
_____

I like myself because
_____
_____
_____

Highlight and why

My part

I like myself because

Highlight and why

My part

I like myself because

Highlight and why

_____

_____

_____

My part

_____

_____

_____

I like myself because

_____

_____

_____

_____

Highlight and why

_____

_____

_____

My part

_____

_____

_____

I like myself because

_____

_____

_____

_____

Highlight and why

_____

_____

_____

My part

_____

_____

_____

I like myself because

_____

_____

_____

Highlight and why

_____

_____

_____

My part

_____

_____

_____

I like myself because

_____

_____

_____

DAY 3

Highlight and why
_____
_____
_____
_____

My part
_____
_____
_____
_____

I like myself because
_____
_____
_____
_____

Highlight and why
_____
_____
_____
_____

My part
_____
_____
_____
_____

I like myself because
_____
_____
_____
_____

Highlight and why

_____

_____

_____

My part

_____

_____

_____

I like myself because

_____

_____

_____

Highlight and why

_____

_____

_____

My part

_____

_____

_____

I like myself because

_____

_____

_____

DAY 4

Highlight and why

_____

_____

_____

My part

_____

_____

_____

I like myself because

_____

_____

_____

_____

Highlight and why

_____

_____

_____

My part

_____

_____

_____

I like myself because

_____

_____

_____

_____

Highlight and why

My part

I like myself because

Highlight and why

My part

I like myself because

DAY 5

Highlight and why

_____

_____

_____

My part

_____

_____

_____

I like myself because

_____

_____

_____

Highlight and why

_____

_____

_____

My part

_____

_____

_____

I like myself because

_____

_____

_____

Highlight and why

_____

_____

_____

My part

_____

_____

_____

I like myself because

_____

_____

_____

_____

Highlight and why

_____

_____

_____

My part

_____

_____

_____

I like myself because

_____

_____

_____

_____

DAY 6

Highlight and why

_____

_____

_____

My part

_____

_____

_____

I like myself because

_____

_____

_____

Highlight and why

_____

_____

_____

My part

_____

_____

_____

I like myself because

_____

_____

_____

Highlight and why

My part

I like myself because

Highlight and why

My part

I like myself because

DAY 7

Highlight and why

_____

_____

_____

My part

_____

_____

_____

I like myself because

_____

_____

_____

_____

Highlight and why

_____

_____

_____

My part

_____

_____

_____

I like myself because

_____

_____

_____

_____

Highlight and why

My part

I like myself because

Highlight and why

My part

I like myself because

DAY 8

Highlight and why

_____

_____

_____

My part

_____

_____

_____

I like myself because

_____

_____

_____

Highlight and why

_____

_____

_____

My part

_____

_____

_____

I like myself because

_____

_____

_____

Highlight and why

My part

I like myself because

Highlight and why

My part

I like myself because

DAY 9

Highlight and why

My part

I like myself because

Highlight and why

My part

I like myself because

Highlight and why

_____

_____

_____

My part

_____

_____

_____

I like myself because

_____

_____

_____

_____

Highlight and why

_____

_____

_____

My part

_____

_____

_____

I like myself because

_____

_____

_____

_____

DAY 10

Highlight and why

_____

_____

_____

My part

_____

_____

_____

I like myself because

_____

_____

_____

_____

Highlight and why

_____

_____

_____

My part

_____

_____

_____

I like myself because

_____

_____

_____

_____

Highlight and why

My part

I like myself because

Highlight and why

My part

I like myself because

DAY 11

Highlight and why

_____

_____

_____

My part

_____

_____

_____

I like myself because

_____

_____

_____

Highlight and why

_____

_____

_____

My part

_____

_____

_____

I like myself because

_____

_____

_____

Highlight and why

My part

I like myself because

Highlight and why

My part

I like myself because

DAY 12

Highlight and why
_____
_____
_____

My part
_____
_____
_____

I like myself because
_____
_____
_____

Highlight and why
_____
_____
_____

My part
_____
_____
_____

I like myself because
_____
_____
_____

Highlight and why

My part

I like myself because

Highlight and why

My part

I like myself because

DAY 13

Highlight and why

_____

_____

_____

My part

_____

_____

_____

I like myself because

_____

_____

_____

Highlight and why

_____

_____

_____

My part

_____

_____

_____

I like myself because

_____

_____

_____

Highlight and why

My part

I like myself because

Highlight and why

My part

I like myself because

DAY 14

Highlight and why
_____
_____
_____
_____

My part
_____
_____
_____
_____

I like myself because
_____
_____
_____
_____

Highlight and why
_____
_____
_____
_____

My part
_____
_____
_____
_____

I like myself because
_____
_____
_____
_____

Highlight and why

My part

I like myself because

Highlight and why

My part

I like myself because

REPEATED THEMES

DELIBERATE ACTION LIST

DAY 15

Highlight and why

_____

_____

_____

My part

_____

_____

_____

I like myself because

_____

_____

_____

Highlight and why

_____

_____

_____

My part

_____

_____

_____

I like myself because

_____

_____

_____

Highlight and why

_____

_____

_____

My part

_____

_____

_____

I like myself because

_____

_____

_____

Highlight and why

_____

_____

_____

My part

_____

_____

_____

I like myself because

_____

_____

_____

DAY 16

Highlight and why
_____
_____
_____

My part
_____
_____
_____

I like myself because
_____
_____
_____

Highlight and why
_____
_____
_____

My part
_____
_____
_____

I like myself because
_____
_____
_____

Highlight and why

_____

_____

_____

My part

_____

_____

_____

I like myself because

_____

_____

_____

Highlight and why

_____

_____

_____

My part

_____

_____

_____

I like myself because

_____

_____

_____

DAY 17

Highlight and why

_____

_____

_____

My part

_____

_____

_____

I like myself because

_____

_____

_____

_____

Highlight and why

_____

_____

_____

My part

_____

_____

_____

I like myself because

_____

_____

_____

_____

Highlight and why

My part

I like myself because

Highlight and why

My part

I like myself because

DAY 18

Highlight and why

_____

_____

_____

My part

_____

_____

_____

I like myself because

_____

_____

_____

Highlight and why

_____

_____

_____

My part

_____

_____

_____

I like myself because

_____

_____

_____

Highlight and why

My part

I like myself because

Highlight and why

My part

I like myself because

DAY 19

Highlight and why
_____
_____
_____

My part
_____
_____
_____

I like myself because
_____
_____
_____

Highlight and why
_____
_____
_____

My part
_____
_____
_____

I like myself because
_____
_____
_____

Highlight and why

My part

I like myself because

Highlight and why

My part

I like myself because

DAY 20

Highlight and why

_____

_____

_____

My part

_____

_____

_____

I like myself because

_____

_____

_____

Highlight and why

_____

_____

_____

My part

_____

_____

_____

I like myself because

_____

_____

_____

Highlight and why

_____

_____

_____

My part

_____

_____

_____

I like myself because

_____

_____

_____

Highlight and why

_____

_____

_____

My part

_____

_____

_____

I like myself because

_____

_____

_____

DAY 21

Highlight and why
_____
_____
_____

My part
_____
_____
_____

I like myself because
_____
_____
_____

Highlight and why
_____
_____
_____

My part
_____
_____
_____

I like myself because
_____
_____
_____

Highlight and why

My part

I like myself because

Highlight and why

My part

I like myself because

DAY 22

Highlight and why

My part

I like myself because

Highlight and why

My part

I like myself because

Highlight and why

My part

I like myself because

Highlight and why

My part

I like myself because

DAY 23

Highlight and why
_____
_____
_____
_____

My part
_____
_____
_____
_____

I like myself because
_____
_____
_____
_____

Highlight and why
_____
_____
_____
_____

My part
_____
_____
_____
_____

I like myself because
_____
_____
_____
_____

Highlight and why

My part

I like myself because

Highlight and why

My part

I like myself because

DAY 24

Highlight and why
_____
_____
_____

My part
_____
_____
_____

I like myself because
_____
_____
_____

Highlight and why
_____
_____
_____

My part
_____
_____
_____

I like myself because
_____
_____
_____

Highlight and why

My part

I like myself because

Highlight and why

My part

I like myself because

DAY 25

Highlight and why

_____

_____

_____

My part

_____

_____

_____

I like myself because

_____

_____

_____

_____

Highlight and why

_____

_____

_____

My part

_____

_____

_____

I like myself because

_____

_____

_____

_____

Highlight and why

_____
_____
_____

My part

_____
_____
_____

I like myself because

_____
_____
_____

Highlight and why

_____
_____
_____

My part

_____
_____
_____

I like myself because

_____
_____
_____

DAY 26

Highlight and why
_____
_____
_____

My part
_____
_____
_____

I like myself because
_____
_____
_____

Highlight and why
_____
_____
_____

My part
_____
_____
_____

I like myself because
_____
_____
_____

Highlight and why

_____

_____

_____

My part

_____

_____

_____

I like myself because

_____

_____

_____

Highlight and why

_____

_____

_____

My part

_____

_____

_____

I like myself because

_____

_____

_____

DAY 27

Highlight and why

My part

I like myself because

Highlight and why

My part

I like myself because

Highlight and why

_____

_____

_____

My part

_____

_____

_____

I like myself because

_____

_____

_____

Highlight and why

_____

_____

_____

My part

_____

_____

_____

I like myself because

_____

_____

_____

DAY 28

Highlight and why
_____
_____
_____
_____

My part
_____
_____
_____
_____

I like myself because
_____
_____
_____
_____

Highlight and why
_____
_____
_____
_____

My part
_____
_____
_____
_____

I like myself because
_____
_____
_____
_____

Highlight and why

My part

I like myself because

Highlight and why

My part

I like myself because

SETTING YOUR SCALE

0/10
_____
_____
_____
_____
_____
_____

10/10
_____
_____
_____
_____
_____

10

Starting Point
_____
_____
_____
_____
_____

0

PROGRESS

Week 1 check in

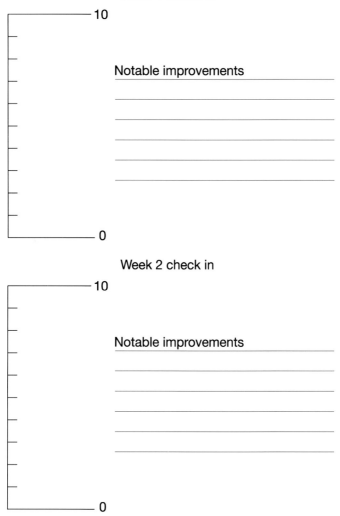

— 10

Notable improvements

_____

_____

_____

_____

_____

_____

— 0

Week 2 check in

— 10

Notable improvements

_____

_____

_____

_____

_____

_____

— 0

PROGRESS
Week 3 check in

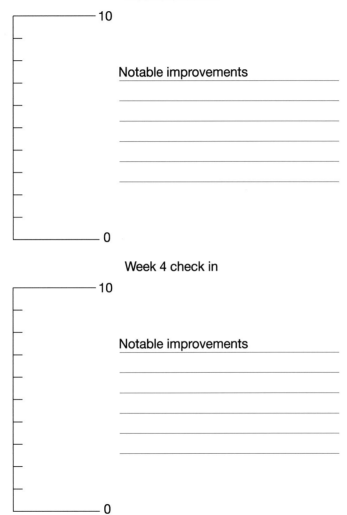

10

Notable improvements

_____

_____

_____

_____

_____

0

Week 4 check in

10

Notable improvements

_____

_____

_____

_____

_____

0

BEFORE

AFTER

BEYOND REBOOT

BEYOND REBOOT

BEYOND REBOOT

BEYOND REBOOT

About George Swift

Many years ago, George was given the nickname, The Mindset Mechanic. He doesn't go by that any more but continues to teach an understanding of what he calls Mindset Mechanics – the mechanical processes of human behaviour. Like a mechanic who knows their way around an engine, when we understand these processes, we can troubleshoot the human mind and work out why it's not firing on all cylinders. Sometimes it only needs a tweak to the tuning, while at others it needs a complete overhaul. George takes complicated neurological processes and psychological concepts and delivers them in a way that makes them easy to consume, digest and, most importantly, apply.

George has a great track record in helping people. He has over 25 years' experience in empowering individuals and teams and improving personal performance. He has been involved in inner-city rejuvenation projects, working with people who live under a constant threat of violence. He's also worked with the Prince's Trust and many high-profile businesses. In 2009, he founded Bigger Brighter Bolder (BBB). By focussing on the mindset, attitudinal, performance and cultural aspects of success, he has coached individuals, CEOs, senior executives, sales people and sports teams to significant levels of achievement.

He has successfully worked with people on their eating disorders, addictions, self-harming, depression, anxiety, violent tendencies and suicidal impulses. He helped them through the process of understanding themselves and how they "tick", allowing them to go on to create happy, successful and fulfilling lives.

He has a passion for entrepreneurism and, in 2012, launched BBB Success Groups for ambitious business owners. He has now coached and mentored over 500 businesses, including start-ups, one-man bands, six-figure businesses and multi-million-pound enterprises.

Having previously struggled with his own confidence and self-esteem for many years, he has first-hand insight into the positive and negative impacts of high and low self-esteem respectively – not just for success, but for happiness, fulfilment and overall quality of life.

It's not the ease of the journey
but our courage and determination to continue
that determines our success.